Casualties

of the

~~Recession~~

Depression

A collection of vignettes
by
Heather Joan Marinos

Casualties of the ~~Recession~~ Depression

Published in the United States by
LEXI Communications, Inc., Miami (Florida).

Library of Congress Cataloging-in-Publication Data
has been applied for.
ISBN 978-0-9887559-0-1 (paperback)
ISBN 978-0-9887559-1-8 (eBook)
Printed in the United States of America
Book design/photos by LEXI Communications, Inc.

TO NICK,

Thank you for navigating the turbulent waters with me.
Και η ιστορία συνεχίζεται, αγάπη μου.

Contents...

...Contents

Introduction

> *"The first panacea for a mismanaged nation is inflation of the currency; the second is war. Both bring a temporary prosperity; both bring a permanent ruin. But both are the refuge of political and economic opportunists."*
>
> ~ Ernest Hemingway

We have been told that the so-called "Great Recession" began in December 2007 and ended in June 2009. Political pundits would have us believe that our economy is on the slow but certain road to recovery. Tell that to the one in seven Americans who, today – in 2013 – survives on food stamps... or the professional who has been unable to find work for well over three years... or the family that lives in a makeshift tent. Yes, indeed, we witnessed the exuberant rise of an American economy and some of us profited handsomely from it, embarking on a spending orgy that knew no limits. But, as with every over-inflated bubble, we knew the day would come when the economy would go bust. And when this happened, it left millions of casualties shattered across the nation. Not to be confused with the chronically poor and homeless demographic, these men and women instead represented a cross-section of the middle class. They were (and still are) the new faces – not of the "Great Recession" – but of a twenty-first century **depression,** one that continues to this day. And, like any progressive malignant tumor, if we continue to deny its existence, the end result will be catastrophic.

There are many economic indicators that are carefully tracked and studied by analysts, when determining the presence of recessions and depressions. Statistics gathered from reputable sources – such as the Bureau of Labor Statistics, the U.S. Census Bureau, and the National Bureau of Economic Research (NBER) – provide a quantitative guide to help economic analysts formulate an educated opinion. However, these statistics are limited, to a degree, by the inability or failure to account for unreported data that inevitably slips through the cracks — such as, for example, the shadow inventory of bank-owned homes that still cannot be accurately accounted for... or the middle-aged professional unable to find a job for a prolonged period of time, spiraling him or her into the quicksand of the chronically unemployed. These factors, and more, make it very difficult to gage – with precision and certainty – whether or not the country is in a recession or a depression.

According to the National Bureau of Economic Research (NBER), a "**recession** is a period between a peak and a trough. During a recession, a significant decline in economic activity spreads across the economy and can last from a few months to more than a year."[1] Although the NBER abstains from separately defining or identifying the term "**depression**," they do point out that the term "**depression** is often used to refer to a particularly severe period of economic weakness. Some economists use it to refer only to the portion of these periods when economic activity is declining. The more common use, however, also encompasses the time until economic activity has returned to close to normal levels."[2] Reasonably speaking, we can all concur that this economic downturn has been both prolonged and severe. However, the more important question is the one that seems to be generating the most dissension: ***"Has economic activity returned to close to normal levels?"***

The short answer is a very emphatic "***No***." It is not normal – not even close – for well-educated, experienced professionals to still find it challenging to secure a job or contract that is commensurate with their level of skills and experience.

It is not normal for multiple cities to file for Chapter 9 bankruptcy protection. Three cities in California (Stockton, San Bernardino and Mammoth Lakes) have already filed, and a fourth city (Atwater) is not far behind.

---

[1] National Bureau of Economic Research (NBER), *Business Cycle Dating Committee*, http://www.nber.org/cycles/recessions.html (January 29, 2013).

[2] National Bureau of Economic Research (NBER), *Business Cycle Dating Procedure: Frequently Asked Questions*, http://www.nber.org/cycles/recessions_faq.html (January 29, 2013).

It is not normal for banks to be so overwhelmed with an unprecedented inventory of foreclosed properties that they allow the defaulted mortgagors to remain living in their homes for sometimes as long as a year after foreclosure judgments have been filed.

It is not normal for cities and counties (nationwide) to lay off police officers and consolidate or close down prisons, to slash costs and stay afloat. Other cost-cutting measures have included reducing the pension benefits for city workers.

And, it is not normal for states to issue IOUs (also known as registered warrants) – in lieu of cash – for tax refunds.[3]

No, economic activity has ***not*** returned to close to normal levels. So, perhaps the time has come to finally upgrade the tropical storm to a hurricane. What has been dubbed the "Great Recession" is, in reality, a depression. To make a literal comparison between this depression and the Great Depression of the 1930s would be to completely miss the mark. Given that we are in the 21st century, we have become dramatically more advanced and sophisticated – economically, and scientifically, technologically, industrially, as a nation and as a people. Therefore, our quantitative and qualitative scales of measurement – in terms of the

---

[3] Jennifer Steinhauer, "Coffers Empty, California Pays With IOUs," *New York Times*, July 3, 2009. (http://www.nytimes.com/2009/07/03/us/03calif.html?pagewanted=all&_r=0).

economy (and in all other areas, for that matter) should reflect these new realities.

This book does not purport to be an economic treatise. It is simply an educated commentary which seeks to highlight the economic issues that continue to plague middle-class America. Reinforced by real-life scenarios of disparate people who hail from states across the nation, the book captures some of their most difficult moments, set against a socio-economic backdrop spanning a period of seven years.

Casting statistical reports aside for the moment, the most compelling evidence comes from the people, themselves. *They* are the casualties of this depression. There are so many stories to tell. It was difficult to keep the selection down to only twenty-three. Theirs span a period commencing in 2006 (when the winds began to shift) and ending in the present day (first quarter of 2013). These are the firsthand accounts of real people, told in short scenes or vignettes – to give the reader a glimpse of some of their challenges and triumphs. Their stories are as inspiring as they are heart-wrenching. Their coping mechanism – in many cases, humor. Their names have been replaced by the generic "he"... "she"... "they" – both to protect their privacy, and also to bring home the point that it could happen to anyone. Including you or me.

They are not losers or deadbeats. They are hard-working, intelligent, middle-class men and women (and, in one vignette, a child) who – for one reason or another – got caught in the eye of the storm. Thankfully, storms do eventually pass. And then the task of rebuilding can begin and, with that, an opportunity to strengthen and reinforce, to learn and grow – so as to preclude such devastation from rearing its ugly head ever again.

2006 - Winds of Change

"The economy depends about as much on economists as the weather does on weather forecasters."

~ Jean-Paul Kauffmann

We all saw it coming. "Commercial Office Space for Rent" signs were cropping up in windows everywhere. Companies were simply not generating enough business to justify the over-inflated cost of office space. One area of business that seemed to be booming, however, was home staging. People were scrambling to sell their homes before the housing market plummeted, so they began hiring home stagers to make their houses more "sellable." By the end of 2006, the housing boom had fizzled – marking the beginning of what would soon become an over-saturated real estate market, full of depreciated homes (with underwater mortgages[4]) gathering dust on the MLS listings.

In Christian E. Weller's report on *The U.S. Economy in*

[4] "Underwater mortgages" — when homeowners are left with more debt on their home than what it is worth on the current market value.

Review: 2006, he summed the year's economy in one word: "slowdown." The report attributed the slowdown (in both job and economic growth) as being "home grown, as consumers saw rising debt payments on the record debt built up in past years," leaving "less money available for key household expenditures... and beginning to push many hardworking families over the edge amid rising loan defaults and bankruptcies." [5]

In reviewing some of the leading economic reports written in 2006, one cannot help shaking one's head in amazement at some of the polar opposite results. On one end of the spectrum, there were the "glass is half empty" economists who believed that the slowdown in employment growth and economic opportunity would inevitably lead the country into a recession. Yet, on the other end, the "glass is half full" economists predicted continued growth for 2007.

If we jump out of 2006 for the moment and look at the present day economic scenario, the debate translates to "*The Great Recession was not a depression and, furthermore, it ended in June 2007. We are now on the road to economic recovery.*" **versus** *"The recession was actually a depression and we're still in it."*

Or, in other words, if it looks like a duck and it quacks like a duck ... it "may" very well be a duck.

---

[5] Christian E. Weller, *The U.S. Economy in Review: 2006*, Center for American Progress, http://www.americanprogress.org/issues/economy/news/2006/12/21/2420/the-u-s-economy-in-review-2006/ (February 4, 2013).

1/*Coffee Shop Blues*

He managed to find a parking spot right in front of the coffee shop, a place he called his "office." As the roar of his Harley died down, he gathered up his bag and went inside. The place was packed, which was unusual for a Wednesday mid-afternoon. He smiled when he saw that his favorite seat by the window was still empty and quickly maneuvered his way in between tables, smiling and nodding at familiar faces – friends, acquaintances and "regulars." It was a northern California melting pot of electrical engineers, lawyers, doctors, architects, professors and entrepreneurs. Many were passionate environmentalists. Quite a few were self-employed consultants like himself, but most of them had day jobs – which was why he was so puzzled that so many were here in the middle of the afternoon.

The mood seemed rather subdued and... something else. But, he couldn't put his finger on what it was. He noticed that several people were just sitting and staring at their computer screens. Others were talking intensely on their cell phones. A few voices were raised.

To the left of him were a group of coffee shop regulars, whom he teasingly called "tree huggers." They were in deep discussion about the negative impact that global warming was having on California, especially the state's agricultural industry. They were saying that heat-trapping emissions, if not significantly reduced in the very near future, would cause major public health issues and could have a devastating effect on California's economy. He couldn't disagree with their arguments. They had reason to be concerned. The past summer had seen one of the worst heat waves in a long time. Severe drought and rampant wildfires were a major concern. Having lost over 20,000 cows and almost a million chickens and turkeys in this last heat wave, the state's dairy industry had requested one billion dollars in disaster relief. And then, of course, there was the problem of the air quality. The environmentalists were shaking their heads sorrowfully. Gazing out the window, he could see the smog in the air. It's only when he drove his Harley through the Santa Cruz Mountains that he could actually smell and breathe some fresh mountain air.

His reverie was interrupted by jarring voices. At the table in front of him were some local businessmen and lawyers. They were talking about Governor Schwarzenegger or, as many liked to joke, "The Governator." This, of course, was a slur born out of the Governor's previous acting role in the movie,"Terminator." The men were embroiled in a heated debate on whether or not he would make the decisions necessary to bring the state's economy back to a healthy level. Most doubted whether he would succeed. The conversation fizzled and the men became silent.

Then he spotted one of his buddies sitting across the room, looking quite grim. Coffee in hand, he went over to his friend's table. It took a few seconds before the guy noticed him standing there. They shook hands and sat down, looking across the table at one another. After a few uncomfortable moments, the man began to speak – his words tumbling out in a fevered rush. Apparently, his friend's consulting contract had just been terminated, making it the third contract in the past year that had gone south (metaphorically-speaking) prematurely. Contract gigs were starting to get scarcer and scarcer in the Valley. His friend was worried about keeping up with the mortgage payments and that he wouldn't be able to provide for his family.

They sat talking for well over an hour. He gave him suggestions and encouragement, in an attempt to boost his morale a bit. Then, he went back to his seat and tried to do some work, but he couldn't concentrate. He felt bad for the guy and, looking around the room, he suddenly figured out what that "something else" was. It was not dissimilar to the tangle of emotions that one experiences after receiving a really bad diagnosis. First, there's the shock. Then, angry denial – followed soon after by fear, worry, and depression. Acceptance is the final emotional process, but there was nothing even close to acceptance in this coffee shop today.

His wife, an optimist to the core, always chided him for being pessimistic. However, what she dubbed "pessimistic," he called "realistic." What he was sniffing in the air today, in this coffee shop filled with a veritable focus group of professionals, was the sharp, bitter smell of Reality. And it wasn't pretty.

2007 - Enter the Drought

> *"When one door closes, another opens; but we often look so long and so regretfully upon the closed door that we do not see the one which has opened for us."*
>
> ~ Alexander Graham Bell

As the nation's (and some would argue, the world's) mecca of high technology innovation, northern California's Silicon Valley is one of the most influential triggers to the rise or fall of the American economy. Silicon Valley, originally named because of the region's reputation (since the early 1970s) for silicon chip innovation, is located in the southern region of the San Francisco Bay area – stretching north of Palo Alto, then over the Santa Cruz Mountains and throughout the city of San Jose and adjacent communities. In the past decade, the Valley has expanded to include the counties of San Mateo, San Francisco and parts of Marin. Silicon Valley's finest include high-tech giants like Adobe Systems, Apple, Cisco Systems, eBay, Google, Hewlett-Packard, Intel, Intuit, LinkedIn, Netflix, Oracle, Twitter and Yahoo – and these just scratch the surface.

Technology booms and busts are all familiar cycles to those who live and work in the Valley. As the golden child of the United States, Silicon Valley is home to some of the world's most brilliant engineers and scientists, daring and innovative entrepreneurs, savvy venture capitalists, and one of the most globally renowned universities – Stanford.

In the 21st century, however, Silicon Valley has been facing some serious challenges that threaten its strength as a world leader in technology innovation. In their report, *2007 Silicon Valley Projections (Tough Challenges – Hopeful Signs)*, the Silicon Valley Leadership Group gives a spot-on summary (in five points) of the Valley's weak spots:

- "The Valley has become one of the costliest places in the United States – and the world – to do business
- Investment in infrastructure, housing stock, and education have lagged the growth and the needs of the population and businesses
- The United States – and the Valley – have not produced the volume of engineering, scientific, math, and other core talent necessary to fuel the high technology engine
- Outsourcing – and offshoring – have blown through the Valley in successive waves of manufacturing, customer service, information technology, and shared services
- Looking at manufacturing, beyond certain capital-intensive and logistics-sensitive processes, manufacturing activity has fled the Valley in waves, to lower cost jurisdictions"[6]

---

[6] Silicon Valley Leadership Group. *2007 Silicon Valley Projections (Tough Challenges — Hopeful Signs).* http://svlg.org/wpcontent/uploads/2011/04/projections_2007.pdf (February 4, 2013).

The ramifications (of these issues) – for Silicon Valley, and for an American economy that is already seriously depressed – are immense. In order to forestall a permanent, seismic shift in Silicon Valley's impact on the nation's economy and on its leadership role in technology innovation, serious attention (and action) must be directed towards resolving these issues. This is not the time to rest on our laurels.

2/The Phones Stopped Ringing

He punched the wall with his fist. He'd been doing that so much lately that his wife kept a container of spackle handy, for drywall touch-ups. His off-site contract would be over by November 30th. Granted, it had lasted longer than he had expected. One year and two months. Pretty good, considering consultant jobs had been waning over the past year or so. This, however, was far from normal. He used to have anywhere from five to seven concurrent contracts. It was a juggling act, to be sure, but he enjoyed the challenging work and didn't mind the long hours. Often, he'd have to turn down client opportunities whenever the agencies called. He'd then refer a few of his colleagues to them. That was back in the days when collaboration was the name of the game – when consultants networked together and referred one another to client opportunities. There had been such an abundance of contract jobs.

Then, the outsourcing trend – that had crept into Silicon Valley some years back – became widespread. Instead of hiring northern California's engineering consultants, renowned for their experience, skill and willingness to work long hours, American companies were now employing tens of thousands of engineers in the Far East, for a small fraction of the American consultant's hourly rate. Furthermore, significant manufacturing was being outsourced to China.

Bangalore (India) was fast becoming a new "Silicon Valley." Just as automobile outsourcing to Japan destroyed Detroit, the outsourcing of high-tech jobs to India and China will cause northern California to suffer a similar fate. He couldn't believe this was happening. Shouldn't America look after its own first? What a disastrous mistake these companies were making! And why? Greed.

He went to check his modem (for the third time that day), to see whether the DSL was working. He glanced at his cell phone. No, there were no missed calls. The silence was disturbing. He made his rounds of networking calls – to his colleagues at the agencies and to some fellow consultants. The news was grim. He heard that one well-known high-tech recruiting agency had recently closed its doors. Not a good sign.

Perhaps it was time for him to explore the idea of diversifying his skills, maybe get a third degree... in another profession.

He shook his head in disbelief. He never thought that engineering consulting would cease to be a viable and profitable profession. Surely he was wrong.

2008 – The Domino Effect

> *"It's heartbreaking to see so many people trapped in a web of enforced idleness, deep debt, and gnawing self-doubt."*
>
> ~ William Jefferson Clinton

There was not much to celebrate as Americans braced themselves to usher in the New Year. An election year, no less. The recession had officially begun in December 2007. And for once, economists were in agreement: the economic prognosis for 2008 was bleak.

Many Americans were unprepared. Unsecured credit card debt was alarmingly high, especially in families where one or both parents were out of work for prolonged periods of time – making it virtually impossible for them to pay their mortgage or rent, let alone to claw their way out of debt.

Extreme financial stress can have a very adverse effect on the human psyche, and on overall health in general. It is difficult to think clearly and act rationally when we are worried about feeding our family or keeping a roof over our head. Anxiety and fear are two very destructive emotions and the havoc that they wreak often cause a domino effect of problems which then trickle down through every aspect of our life.

In its 2008 *Stress in America*[7] survey results, the American Psychological Association reports that women (especially the Baby Boomers aged 44-63) have been the most affected, emotionally and physically, from the financial stress of this economic downturn. According to APA's Director for Professional Practice, Dr. Katherine Nordal: "Many say they are handling their stress well. Yet, people report more physical and emotional symptoms. If Americans continue to experience these high levels of stress for prolonged periods of time, they are at risk for developing serious illnesses."[8] The survey data cited a wide range of physical and emotional symptoms caused by stress, such as: depression, increased alcohol consumption, smoking, headaches, insomnia, fatigue, irritability, lack of motivation, muscle tension, high blood pressure, and overeating (especially junk foods).

Extreme financial trauma ravages the soul and ages the body prematurely. Faces do not lie. They bear the scars of intense stress – scars that cannot easily be erased.

---

[7] American Psychological Association. *Stress in America 2008,* http://www.apa.org/news/press/releases/2008/10/stress-in-america.pdf (February 6, 2013).

[8] American Psychological Association. *APA Poll Finds Women Bear Brunt of Nation's Stress, Financial Downturn,* http://www.apa.org/news/press/releases/2008/10/stress-women.aspx (February 6, 2013).

3/A Dead Bluebird

"What a lovely Christmas we had," she thought to herself as she sipped her glass of wine. She had to hold her glass carefully so that the turbulence wouldn't cause an unwelcome accident. She and her husband were flying back to their "home away from home." Yes, the holidays had been very enjoyable, although a bit subdued. Nevertheless, she hadn't minded. Her husband, on the other hand, was a bit tense. She kept assuring him that there will be more consulting contracts in the New Year. He gave her that scrunched-up facial expression which conveyed that he thought she was talking a load of nonsense. She winked back at him, trying to lighten the mood. It didn't work. So, she went back to sipping her Cabernet and enjoying the company of her own thoughts.

After they arrived home, unpacked and freshened up, they went up to their property to make sure that nothing was amiss. Behind the cabin they always kept big white buckets, to collect rainwater. She almost walked passed them when something caught her eye and she stopped so quickly that she nearly stumbled down the cliff. She called to her husband. He came to see what she was pointing at. It was a dead bluebird, floating face down in one of the pails of water. The bird was completely intact. Its wings, with beautiful deep blue and indigo plumage, were spread out. In silence, both husband and wife made the sign of the cross. It was an automatic gesture of respect and mourning that they did whenever they saw a dead animal. They had a special affinity for birds, though. There is much symbolism associated with these feathered creatures and, being slightly superstitious, they believed that a dead bird was a bad omen. It symbolized death. They both looked at each other and knew what the other was thinking: This was not a good start to the year.

They gently wrapped the bird in a napkin and placed him on the cabin's rooftop, a ritual that they did whenever they found a dead bird. The idea behind it was that they were sending the bird up to the heavens, and to God.

As they drove back to the house, neither one spoke.

Twelve days later, they received a phone call at 10:30 pm. It was one of their closest family friends calling to tell them that her husband had died suddenly that day. He was only 51.

Their year began with a funeral and no contract job in sight. The "Recession" had begun. Hopefully, it would pass quickly.

4/Winged Messenger

She lifted her head from the pillow when she heard the noise. Tap-tap-tap. The staccato tapping was barely audible, but persistent. The sound seemed to be coming from outside the front door. Then, it stopped. She didn't hear any footsteps on the landing, so she decided that she must have been dreaming. She snuggled under the down comforter and went back to sleep. It was 6:30 am.

About an hour later, her slumber was interrupted again – by more gentle tapping at the door. Her curiosity got the better of her so she stretched, stood up, and then shuffled to the front door. Looking through the peep hole, she found herself eye-to-eye with a little sparrow. He tilted his head sideways so that he could get a better look. Blue eye met brown eye. He hopped around her wreath and then flew away. "How odd!" she thought to herself. Now, one could point out that he was probably attracted to the wreath and was trying to gather material for a nest. However, her apartment was located up on the third floor and although the stairwell and landings were outside, they were enclosed. Birds never made their way up there. Ever. The stray cats did, but not the birds. She shrugged and smiled to herself, and then went to put the kettle on.

Later that day, she went down to get the mail. There were lots of bills that she didn't know how she would pay, but not one check from her clients (who were very late in paying her because they were in a financial crunch themselves). She almost didn't notice the ivory-colored envelope bearing a university crest. When she did, her hands started to shake. She ripped open the envelope and scanned the letter quickly. Then she squealed. And twirled around. Some habits survive well past childhood. She had been accepted into the PhD program, and at the university that was on the top of her preferred list!

It was going to be an expensive endeavor. Some of her friends thought that she was crazy to even consider it. She would be racking up the student loans – with interest. Nevertheless, she was convinced that this was the thing to do. Education was an investment in the future. Short term pain for long term gain. Her consulting business was simply not yielding anything right now. This was the time to do something totally different.

"Diversify. Diversify. Diversify." This was her new mantra.

She poured herself a glass of wine, knowing that it was a luxury that she will no longer be able to afford. She raised her glass in a silent toast to herself and then stopped, mid-sip. The sparrow! Could it be that he had been tapping on her door to tell her that good news was finally coming her way? She laughed out loud, thinking that she had better ease up on the wine.

But, who knows? Stranger things have happened.

5/And the Juggling Act Begins

Her home office was a mess. Her friend looked around the room in shock and then watched her frantically sifting through the clutter, in search of a Wall Street Journal article that she had clipped and put aside. She was normally a neat freak so he knew that something was really off. He grabbed her arms, to stop her and then he made her sit down, noticing the beads of perspiration forming on her forehead. She saw his eyes wander to her forehead and spat out the words "hot flashes."

"My world is falling to pieces. I'm in debt up to my eyeballs and, damn it, I am just now going through Menopause. Great timing, isn't it? I'm only forty-three! I can feel my bones going brittle as we speak. I can't think straight. My blood pressure is through the roof. I'm angry and hyper all the time...," she started to hiccup sob. He knelt down in front of her until they were at the same eye level and touched his forehead against hers. "This time will pass," he said. "I promise. Everything will be all right and someday, it will be a distant memory. You will become wiser for having had this experience." She calmed down a bit, but looked unconvinced.

He suggested that they tidy up her office and then sort through all her bills. She found the article she had been searching for, and showed it to him. It was about how to prepare for a recession. One of the suggestions was to stock up on credit cards, so that – if need be – they could be used if/when cash flow problems occurred. He shook his head and looked at her like a schoolteacher admonishing a child. He knew far too many people who were living off their lines of credit because they had no work and had gone through all their savings. And, when all the lines of credit run out... what then? He looked at his friend's stack of bills. She had amassed a grand total of fourteen (14) credit cards! Her debt load was almost $150K. She was trying to keep up with all the minimum payments, but she was losing track of how many bills she had and how much credit left in each card. She was paying one off with the other, hoping that she had calculated correctly. All that pressure was clearly taking some toll on her. Physically, she looked at least ten years older than she was. She was sleep-deprived. Emotionally, she was completely messed up, clearly overwhelmed and paralyzed with worry. Worse, her logic was impaired. She was in need of some serious guidance – a Come-to-Jesus type of meeting.

He went to her kitchen and fixed her a sandwich and some tea. He brought it to her and said that he would have to step out for a minute, to go to the nearby health food store. Fifteen minutes later, he came back with some Melatonin (a natural sleep aid). He filled a glass of water and told her to take a capsule and go to bed. He would sit down and figure out a plan to help her sort things out. She did as she was told and went up to her room. He brushed his fingers through his hair, rolled up his sleeve cuffs and sat down at her desk.

It took about five hours, but it was time well-spent. He sorted out all her bills and organized everything on a spreadsheet. He prepared a bill schedule for her. And, he made a few long calls. One of his friends was a credit counselor. He made an appointment for her to meet with the counselor the next day, to determine how the debts could be consolidated and the interest rates reduced. Of course, that would mean that she would have to have a regular stream of income. He made three appointments for her, with recruiters. If she didn't get a job soon, the debts could not be consolidated and she may have to file for bankruptcy. Not a palatable option, to be sure, but if she's backed into a corner, that's what would inevitably have to happen. Hopefully, it wouldn't come to that.

She woke up to the mouthwatering smell of spaghetti Bolognese, her favorite. There he was, that dear fellow, uncorking a bottle of Chianti. The table was set and a feast of spaghetti, salad and bread was waiting to be enjoyed. He winked at her and said "Let's give those brittle bones some nourishment." She laughed so hard that tears welled in her eyes. Good tears, this time.

They sat down and she looked across the table at him with deep affection and gratitude. "Thank you," she whispered. He smiled his response.

6/Shutting Down

"WhatamIgoingtodo... whatamIgoingtodo... whatamIgoingtodo?!"

He spoke his words manically, in hollow breaths, while pacing back and forth and around his dining room table. He felt the walls closing in on him. He hadn't shaved, showered or changed clothes in three days. The night before, he and his wife had the mother of all fights. They were always fighting these days, but this one was bad. He prayed that their little daughter had slept through the angry voices. Normally a bubbly and mischievous child, she had become very quiet lately. He wished he could shield her from all of this, but that was proving to be impossible.

The retail business that he built from scratch fifteen years ago, had gone bust. He tried everything he could to save it. In doing so, he got a second mortgage on his house. Big mistake.

The doors of his business closed for good last Friday. He had to let go of 35 employees – people with families of their own, people whom he considered "family." He had let them down. He had let his wife and child down. He felt like such a Loser. They were in danger of losing their home and everything in it. There had been a few heart-stopping letters from the bank and some really nasty calls and letters from other creditors. The future was not looking good.

He had considered suicide, but he knew he could never go through with it. He was a practicing Catholic. It would devastate his family. He knew that his wife still loved him deeply. She was just as frustrated as he was, but more verbal about it. He kept his emotions all bottled up, except when he was alone in the house, like now. Well, sort of alone. Everyone was in bed, fast asleep.

He slumped to the floor. He noticed his daughter's rubber ball nearby. He snatched it and began throwing it against the wall. Thump, thump. Thump, thump. He didn't stop. His mind was full of what could best be described as graffiti. For some strange reason, he thought of that scene in the movie, Fatal Attraction – when Glenn Close's character sat on the floor of her bedroom. Listening to that Puccini opera, Madame Butterfly, she kept turning the light switch on and off, on and off – while staring into space. That was exactly how he felt right now.

He needed some air. He went out to the back porch and sat on the steps. Then, he held his head in his hands, bent into his knees, and sobbed.

7/Downsizing for Money

She felt that everyone in the store was looking at her. Perhaps she was being overly sensitive, but when she looked back at them, they quickly averted their eyes. Except for one woman. Dressed in head-to-toe Chanel and heavy make-up, the woman stared back at her with a look of barely veiled contempt. The jewelry store owner, sensing her embarrassment, kindly shielded the view and very quickly assessed all the gold jewelry that she was selling to him. Over the years, she had gathered quite a lovely collection of jewelry. However, the thought of giving up all her crosses made her sick to her stomach. They were precious to her. Every cross pendant that she owned, she was being forced to sell. She needed to gather things, to sell off, before they were taken from her. At least she and her family (husband and young daughter) would have a little cash on hand. God knows how long it would last.

The jewelry store owner handed her $850. This was in exchange for five cross pendants, four bracelets, ten pairs of earrings, two necklaces and four rings — all 18K to 24K gold. She looked at him, shocked. He shrugged and she noticed a shrewd look in his eye. He smelled her desperation and, like all predators, decided that he would take advantage of her vulnerability. He *lifted an eyebrow, as if to say "Well, take it or leave it... what's it going to be?" She bit the inside of her cheek. She wanted to tell him to go to hell, but knew that the $850 would help her family. She gave him a disgusted look and thought "If there is such a thing as Karma, may it please bite him in the ass one day." She took the money and left the store quickly, not glancing back.*

She walked fast, for about ten blocks. She was angry and heartbroken. The tears began to stream down her face. She felt ashamed at being reduced to this. Her tears dried by the time she arrived home. Her neighbor waved to her with a smile. She waved back. In her neighbor's eyes, she saw kindness and understanding. She would be sad to leave this place. Then, she saw her beautiful, five-year-old darling sitting on the porch steps. And, just like that, her child's smile erased the memory of the day's unpleasantness. They walked into the house, hand-in-hand.

Tomorrow, three people were coming over to buy some furniture. They had each responded to her ads on Craigslist. She leaned against the kitchen sink, her arms spread out on the counter, and looked out the window. A hummingbird fluttered above the flower pot on her window sill. She smiled. Her spirits lifted.

"We will get through this, somehow," she promised herself.

8/ *Through the Eyes of a Child*

She skittered behind the stairwell and sat down. With her arms wrapped tightly around her knees, she watched through the space between the stairs. Her long ash blonde hair cascaded around her like a shawl. Her clear, blue eyes were wide and close to tears. The lady who lived next door was talking with her mother and as they passed by the stairs, the lady spotted her and smiled. She put her finger up to her nose silently. The lady understood and didn't tell her mother that she was hiding under the stairs. They went into the next room.

She hadn't seen her father all morning. The night before, her parents had a terrible fight. They were always fighting. But last night was the worst. They had been yelling at one another and then she heard her mother crying. She had buried her face in the pillow, to block out the sounds. After awhile, everything went quiet. From her bedroom window, she heard a noise on the back porch. She looked out and down, towards the porch, and saw that her father was sitting on the steps. She wiggled out of bed and tip-toed downstairs. She opened the screen door just enough so that she could see him better. He was bent over with his hands around his head. He was making a sound that she had never heard before. Daddy was crying! She had never seen her Daddy cry before. Things must be terribly wrong. Her heart started beating fast. She covered her mouth to stifle a cry. Quietly, she closed the door and went back upstairs to her room. She cried herself to sleep.

This morning, her mother told her to stay out of the way because men were coming to take all their furniture and things away. She didn't understand why. There were four of them. Big and sweaty, they were taking things out of the house. Nobody noticed her behind the stairwell. She saw them take her princess canopy bed away. Her mouth began to tremble and she bit her lip, to keep from crying. A big man with no hair came out of her playroom, carrying her toy box and on top of the box was her favorite American Girl® Doll, Caroline. Caroline had blonde hair and blue eyes, just like her. She gasped. The big man heard her. He turned around and bent down slightly, squinting his eyes. Then, he spotted her. He saw her staring at the doll on top of the box that he was carrying. He started to turn away towards the front door, but her tear-stained face and big blue eyes stopped him. He looked around. No one else was in sight, or so he thought. Quickly, he grabbed the doll and slid it under the stairs. He put his fingers to his lips, "Shhh..." and gave her a wink. Then he was gone. She grinned from ear to ear and clutched Caroline to her chest.

She heard a noise and looked up. The lady next door extended her hand. She put her hand in the neighbor's and, holding Caroline tightly, she got up from under the stairs. The lady called out to her mother and said that she would take her (and Caroline) next door for some tea and cake. She and the lady had always enjoyed their little tea parties together. She would miss the kind lady when they moved.

As they left the house, she saw the man with no hair. She gave him a shy smile and he looked at her. His eyes were soft and wet. "Maybe he's coming down with a cold," she thought.

2009 – The Sky is Falling

> *"I've seen dreams that move the mountains, hope that doesn't ever end, even when the sky is falling.*
> *I've seen miracles just happen, silent prayers get answered, broken hearts become brand new...*
> *That's what faith can do."*
>
> ~ Kutless (Christian rock band) - from the song *"What Faith Can Do"*

As long as we are able to breathe, then there will always be hope – even when it feels like our lives are taking a free fall dive into Hell. So, what does Hell look like these days? Never a destination of choice, Hell is when we find ourselves without a job for what seems like forever, living in that van down by the river (instead of a home) and surviving on a monthly stipend of food stamps.

2009 was the year from hell. And if one more economist or politician goes on television to spout the standard nonsensical rhetoric that the so-called "Great Recession" ended in June 2009, a flying shoe will be thrown at the TV screen. Of course, for the hundreds of thousands of Americans whose cable has been cut off due to unpaid bills... well, they have been spared the affront. Maybe there is a bright side to financial ruin, after all.

The year 2009 began with 11.6 million people unemployed, and the number of jobs lost (between December 2007 and January 2009) reached a staggering 3.2 million.[9] Many more job losses were expected to (and did) follow.

On the home front, a record 2.82M homes faced foreclosure in 2009. In its *U.S. Foreclosure Market Report™ for Q3 2009*, RealtyTrac® stated that foreclosure filings increased by 23% since Q3 2008.[10] Homelessness was fast becoming a middle-class phenomenon – or, to be more precise, a nightmare. The National Coalition for the Homeless issued a strong recommendation in its Joint Report, *Foreclosure to Homelessness 2009: the Forgotten Victims of the Subprime Crisis*:

> "It is imperative that federal and state governments, in collaboration with local communities, prioritize preventing homelessness while also assisting those who have already become homeless. People must have immediate access to safe shelter and be rapidly re-housed within the community. Priority should be given to reusing foreclosed homes and rental properties by making them available - either to the current occupants through rent-back or stabilization agreements or through

---

[9] U.S. Department of Labor, Bureau of Labor Statistics, The Editor's Desk, *Increase in unemployment rate in January 2009,* http://www.bls.gov/opub/ted/2009/feb/wk2/art02.htm (February 6, 2013).

[10] RealtyTrac®, *U.S. Foreclosure Market Report™ for Q3 2009,* http://www.realtytrac.com/foreclosure/foreclosure-rates.html (February 6, 2013).

> incentives for the donation or sale of the property to non-profits for use by persons living on very low incomes. It is only through a multi-dimensional approach that takes a spectrum of human needs into account, and considers them in context with the economic climate of our country, that we will be able to bring America home." [11]

In tandem with the rise in foreclosures and homelessness, was the rising number of households that were experiencing varying degrees of "food insecurity" – a term coined by the U.S. Department of Agriculture. Many middle-class families, finding themselves in this new and foreign predicament, began to participate in the private pantry programs cropping up across the nation. The premise behind the concept of "private pantry" is that food, household items and toiletries get donated regularly to these private pantries and those needing assistance can go in there and gather food for their families, while maintaining their privacy and dignity.

Human dignity. Is it not our basic entitlement?

---

[11] National Coalition for the Homeless et al., *Foreclosure to Homelessness 2009: the forgotten victims of the subprime crisis (p.14)*, http://www.nationalhomeless.org/advocacy/ForeclosuretoHomelessness0609.pdf (February 6,2013).

9/*Homeless in Canvas*

They sat in folding chairs, across from one another. They both looked like they had just been sucker punched. Each knew what the other was thinking. "How in the hell did this happen?!" They looked around at the seven roller suitcases and five large plastic storage boxes containing all their "worldly goods" – downsized from a 2500 square foot home, a home that the bank had foreclosed on eight months earlier. "Downsizing" was a word they had grown to despise. They both had been "downsized" from their respective jobs. They were 58-years old. They were looking for work, but so was everyone else. The few available jobs went to the younger ones. Yes, ageism was alive and well, and living in California.

After they lost their home, they rented a motel room because their poor credit rating prohibited them from renting an apartment. When money began to run out, they started sleeping in their SUV. However, when they could no longer pay for gas and when the confines of tight space had begun to give them some health issues from a lack of proper leg circulation, they were forced to find alternative living arrangements.

They could hear a couple arguing in a tent nearby. The stench of vomit became more intense. The young woman, who lived in a small pup tent across theirs, was three months pregnant and had a bad case of morning sickness. A dog barked incessantly in the distance.

They hadn't eaten since yesterday afternoon, but they weren't hungry. It's hard to have an appetite when you find yourself reduced to living in a tent city.

They didn't tell friends and relatives about their predicament. Not even their grown children, who lived back East. They didn't want charity or handouts. They had been used to a nice middle-class life, with a household income of $145K per year. They hadn't thought ahead. That was their critical mistake. And now they were paying for it.

No, they were too proud and ashamed. It is interesting how pride and shame, contradictory by definition, can coexist so seamlessly.

There was a rumor that government officials and law enforcement were going to force everyone to evacuate. It didn't look good to have a tent city in the area. The idea was to shift the "problem" to some other location. Problem. They had never imagined that one day they would be referred to as a "problem."

They moved their chairs closer to each other and clasped hands. They'd lived through what seemed like a lifetime together, here in California. Perhaps it was time to move eastward. They didn't want to be in a place where they were made to feel like human garbage.

They opened the cooler and chuckled. One luxury remained. It was a small box of Godiva truffles that they had squirreled away for a rainy day. As they savored the dark chocolate delights, they smiled. It's uncanny how a few bites of chocolate always manage to uplift the spirit.

10/*Gee, Thanks for the Pink Slip*

He was surprised at how calm he felt as he packed the personal belongings from his office. He looked around, pleased that he had been correct in calculating that he would only need three boxes. He put his jacket and hat on. It was a rather frosty January, even by northern California standards. His boss had waited until after the Christmas and New Year holidays, to give him the news. His job had been eliminated. He wondered to himself whether it was kinder to give someone the pink slip before, or after Christmas. If he had known he was going to be unemployed, he probably wouldn't have been so extravagant with the Christmas gifts that he bought for his siblings, nieces and nephews. Oh, well. What's done is done.

He walked passed the receptionist, who gave him a sad look. She was taken aback when he winked at her. He chuckled under his breath.

Strangely enough, he was neither upset nor depressed. He actually felt.... relieved. By nature, he was not a melancholic, the-cup-is-half-empty kind of person. He was pragmatic, confident and, yes, (let's call a spade a spade) – charming. He grinned to himself. His mind was already churning with all sorts of ideas and plans for the future.

He was going to reinvent himself. America is home to millions of people who reinvent themselves all the time. They fall down, pick themselves up, dust off the debris of Yesterday, and then prepare for an even better Tomorrow.

When he arrived home, he threw the boxes on the floor and went to take a shower. Refreshed, he opened his humidor and picked a nice Arturo Fuente cigar, then poured himself a glass of Macallan 18 year single malt scotch. On the way to his favorite club chair, he flipped a switch and the jazzy sounds of Miles Davis filled the room.

Yes, he should probably thank his boss for firing him. Truth be told, he was feeling stagnant in his role as Director for a company that wasn't very forward-thinking.

This was, in fact, the kick in the butt that he truly needed.

He was excited for tomorrow.

11/The Kindness of Strangers

She walked briskly out of the supermarket. The aisles of food and the smell of fresh fruit and vegetables had made her light-headed. She had spent two dollars on a dozen eggs and some bread and only had ten dollars left in her purse – in quarters. She passed by a man who was standing near a bench by the store entrance. He was tall, thin, about thirty-something, dressed in clean jeans and a t-shirt, and was African American. He was asking people for money to buy some food. She glanced at him, mumbled "Sorry, I can't" and continued walking.

Then, something in her sub-conscious made her stop and turn around. He was sitting on the bench, his head in his hands. She noticed something that she recognized only too well. Despair. She reached into her purse and counted five dollars worth of quarters (half of what she had left to last her for the next two weeks) and she walked back to the man and said "Excuse me sir, but here is five dollars in quarters. I hope this will help tide you over." He looked at her. She could hear the intake of his breath. His eyes were clear and intelligent. He stood up and thanked her, very earnestly and with respect. Their eyes met and he understood. They were the same.

12/*Life in a Storage Unit*

It was a steamy South Florida midsummer day and they just loaded the last of their stuff in the truck. Really, they had way too much stuff. Accumulated over 30+ years, they had about two households worth of things.... and that was excluding what was already in their current home. This was the last truckload going to their storage unit, an 8' x 20' air-conditioned space with high ceilings. The thought did cross their minds that maybe they should sell or give away a lot of it, but they kept putting it off for mañana.

They didn't want their possessions to weigh them down, to keep them from being mobile. So, they opted for a storage unit. For many households, storage units were an extension of their garage. What they couldn't store at home, due to space restrictions, spilled over to their rented storage bays.

There was an alarming trend spreading quickly throughout middle-class America. People were losing their homes, through foreclosure or bankruptcy (or both), and so they rented storage units to protect what little they had left... until they were no longer able to pay the monthly storage rent. And then their belongings, their "Life," would wind up in a rubble thrown unceremoniously into the storage company's dumpsters – either to be sold off by the storage company, pillaged by junk collectors, or to be picked up by the sanitation department.

When they dropped off their last load into their storage unit, they saw a stuffed animal – a giraffe – on the ground, next to the dumpster. There were more toys and household items filling up the container. They felt sad, knowing for certain that some child's beloved toys were surely casualties of unpaid storage.

As they walked through the row of storage bays, something caught their eye and made them stop. In one of the units, there was an older woman who was sitting in a well-worn armchair. She was drinking a glass of iced tea. When she noticed them she quickly closed the sliding bay door, afraid that they would squeal on her. They looked at each other in shock. Was she actually living there? Their eyes spoke the question and their suspicions were confirmed when they noticed another storage bay with a man and a boy. Father and son were sitting on folding chairs, eating some fast food and both looked up at them defiantly... staring them down.

They finally reached their car and quickly went in. They looked at each other sideways, still reeling from what they had just witnessed. When they arrived back home, they felt an enormous sense of relief and gratitude for the many blessings that they had in their life. They also made a vow to themselves that they would make it a priority to go through all their excess "stuff" and give it away to people who needed it more.

13/*Young and Hungry*

He sat in the coffee shop, his fingers restlessly turning the pages of his textbook. He had been there for three and a half hours, nursing a cup of coffee. "Thank God for free refills!" – he thought to himself. He was trying hard to focus on the words in front of him, willing the gurgling in his empty stomach to go away. His hands were slightly shaky. He could smell the toasted ham and cheese sandwich that someone was eating at a nearby table. Freshly baked bread had just come out of the oven and the lady behind the counter was stacking the loaves on the shelf. His mouth started to water and he felt dizzy. He willed himself to block it all out. Two more hours passed by.

It was closing time. The coffee shop lady was rushing to close up. She grabbed all the leftover loaves of bread (two were left), bagels (all seven of them), and two donuts – and threw them roughly into a big garbage can, which she wheeled into the back room. He swallowed, throat dry. A tear escaped from the corner of his eye. He was too proud to ask. And the coffee shop lady didn't see, nor would she probably have given him a second thought if she had. He clenched his jaw and grimly packed his book into his bag.

He glanced once at the lady behind the counter. Her face was blank when she looked back at him. Oblivious. She tapped her fingers on the glass, impatient to close the lights.

He left quietly, not looking back. He wondered whether things would get better after he graduated from college. He wasn't so sure.

(**PS:** This coffee shop actually went out of business and closed its doors for good, just one month later. And the fate of the lady behind the counter? She joined the ranks of the unemployed.)

14/*Ringing off the Hook*

She looked down at her cell phone. Twenty-eight missed calls. She scrolled through the numbers. They were all creditors. The calls had begun at 8:00 am that day. She looked at the clock. It was 6 pm. There would be more by 9:00 pm. She couldn't answer the calls because, if she did, she would be cajoled into making payment arrangements that she would not be able to keep up. Her income was sporadic, at best. Until things got better financially, she would have to keep the creditors at bay and pray that things wouldn't get too nasty.

There were so many letters. She kept a spreadsheet, which she updated at the end of each month. It listed the original creditor and the creditor who had purchased the debt. In some cases, the debts had gone through three or four purchasing cycles. The interest was a strange, and often erratic, anomaly. It seemed to skyrocket and then magically shrink, at the whim of the latest creditor. She couldn't figure out whether they were scamming her or not. This was not an area of expertise that she would ever dream of delving into. Nevertheless, it was her intention to pay all of her debts, when her income became regular and substantial enough to make settlements, to pay them off at once. She was not a deadbeat. People always seemed to judge others so quickly. "Did it ever occur to them that sometimes shit happens? " she muttered out loud. She hadn't expected the economic downturn to effectively annihilate her business. Several substantial contracts had been terminated, due to insufficient resources and so, they could no longer honor their agreements with the consultants. It was a domino effect that was spiraling out of control.

It used to be that the phone would be ringing off the hook from the many job recruiters who called about available contract jobs, now it's the creditors who are calling. A sign of the times.

She was working on a way to diversify her company. She had to do something. She was 39-years old. The clock was ticking. She didn't want to live this nightmare indefinitely.

Yes, she would pay each one of those creditors, but there was no way that she was going to pay that trumped-up interest.

The down side was that, by defaulting on her creditors, she had a bad credit rating. The up side was that she didn't have any more credit cards. It was a weird, yet freeing feeling.

Cash only. Her father had been right. Sometimes the old ways were better.

She lifted her cup of tea in a silent toast to her dad, "Here's to living frugally!"

15/Out of Retirement

He didn't like his wife's pallor. It was pale and pasty. He touched her forehead and noticed that it was clammy. She had just completed an eight-week round of chemo. Fifteen years ago, they found out that she had breast cancer. His wife had been devastated when she was told that she would have to have a radical mastectomy. He had been terrified, but had tried to put on a brave face for her. They weathered that storm together, the way they always did when life threw a few bumps their way. Married for 47 years, he couldn't fathom what his world would be like without her in it.

Eight years ago, the doctors found a malignant tumor in her uterus and recommended a hysterectomy. And, of course, more chemotherapy. They dealt with that, as well. But all the medical bills had taken their toll on their savings. Their vision of retirement included buying a second home somewhere in Europe. His preference was for Tuscany, hers was for Paris. He would give the world to her if he could, so Paris it would be.

However, the second cancer changed everything. Their savings had dwindled. Their insurance premiums were ridiculously high. The previous year, they were forced to reverse mortgage their home, so as to keep up with their medical bills. Now, the bank owned it and they get to live in it (for "free") for the duration of their lives, after which time the house would revert to the bank.

Recently, they learned that the breast cancer has returned. He couldn't understand how it could be breast cancer since she had a mastectomy years ago. Whether he understood it all or not, it was back – with a vengeance. He wasn't so sure that she would survive this one. Hell, he didn't know whether he would survive.

They had no more savings. He would have to find a job, although he knew that would be a challenge. Jobs were scarce. And he was 68. If he did manage to find work, it would mean spending time away from his wife. They had so few precious moments left.

She stirred in her bed. She looked up at him with a smile that reached her eyes. He knew the pain that the smile cost her. She whispered "Let's listen to some music. Not too loud, though, please." He put her favorite Edith Piaf CD in the player and went to sit beside her. They held hands and gazed at each other, as "La Vie en Rose" played softly in the background.

2010 – Still Standing... Just

"You never really understand a person until you consider things from his point of view - until you climb into his skin and walk around in it."

~ spoken by Atticus Finch, *To Kill a Mockingbird*, by Harper Lee

The true test of friendship and family is not when things are all rosy and nice, but when times are hard. All too often, the rockier the ride gets, the more people want to jump out at the first possible exit. There will always be fair-weather friends, and family members who don't comprehend the true meaning of family. A person's need for a sympathetic ear, a sounding board or objective advice and guidance should not immediately be construed as being a disguised request for financial handouts. More often than not, it has nothing at all to do with money. It usually has *everything* to do with the human spirit and the need to be uplifted – especially during difficult times.

There's almost always a silver lining. When all the onion layers are peeled off, we find out which people we want to keep in our lives and which ones we must distance ourselves from. And, as we move forward, we treasure the people who have weathered the storm with us and anticipate sharing good times together, when the sun comes out once again.

The late Malcolm S. Forbes once said, "When things are bad, we take comfort in the thought that they could always be worse. And when they are, we find hope in the thought that things are so bad, they have to get better."

From your lips to God's ears, Mr. Forbes.

16/Kick Us When We're Down

His knuckles were taut as he clenched the steering wheel. He stared fixedly at the long stretch of highway ahead of him. He was livid. Greed, jealousy, selfishness and lack of collaboration. The words described his family in a nutshell. Blessed (or cursed) with a photographic memory, he suddenly remembered a quote from his favorite Ayn Rand novel, The Fountainhead – just as a tailgater nearly rammed into his car. He switched lanes. It was about money. Rand wrote that: "Money is only a means to some end. If a man wants it for a personal purpose — to invest in his industry, to create, to study, to travel, to enjoy luxury — he's completely moral. But the men who place money first, go much beyond that. Personal luxury is a limited endeavor. What they want is ostentation: to show, to stun, to entertain, to impress others... at the price of their own self-respect." That fit a few family members to a tee.

For sure, money can be very divisive. Toxic, even. It is one of the leading causes of family conflict, friendship break-up, and divorce. It shouldn't be, but we let it be. He shook his head and slammed one fist on the dash. His parents were probably rolling over in their graves. His eyes welled as he thought of his parents. They had meant well when they bequeathed all their assets, in equal shares, to their children. What they didn't anticipate was the hornet's nest that their good intentions created.

With each sibling's family came a unique personal agenda. Some wanted to sell shares. Others wanted to buy out the shares. And a few wanted to keep everything as it always was, out of respect to their parents' memory. The characters were diverse. Some were seemingly friendly yet wily, others were elusive, a few were volatile and irrational, and the remaining ones were logical, though sentimental.

This would not end well.

Each of the siblings had been adversely affected by the recession, in one way or another. One family (his) was suffering a series of dramatic economic setbacks that were completely alien to them because they had always been so financially stable and secure.

And what happens when vultures see a creature that is wounded and vulnerable? They swoop down for the kill, that's what. The difference is that some humans, unlike vultures, wear smiles on their faces... shed crocodile tears of sympathy, and they offer acts of kindness... but, for a price – with interest and unreasonable conditions attached. And, if you don't comply... bam! A lawsuit is filed. And another. And another.

He got off the exit ramp. He had learned his lessons

well. His family of siblings had eroded. He was friendly with some. Others, he no longer considered family.

His local priest once said, in a Christmas sermon: "For those of you who have estranged family members, try to keep the door open... just a wee bit." Unfortunately, he planned on keeping the door firmly shut. Some things cannot be forgiven.

Then he remembered another quote. This one was from the Kung Fu TV series (circa 1970s), where David Carradine's character, Kwai Chang Caine, said to a fellow Shaolin priest who had just betrayed him for money: "A Shaolin monk does not sell himself for a handful of rice."

17/ *Just in the Nick of Time*

Never in a million years would she have imagined that she would be facing foreclosure. She had owned her apartment for twenty years. It was completely paid for, free and clear – no mortgage, no equity loans. The past year had been unusually rough. She had to close down her advertising firm. She had been losing business steadily for a while now. Advertising was a budget line item that was always the first to be slashed when a company began to cut costs. In this recession, advertising was a luxury, not a necessity.

She was cash poor. This was a very foreign and unpleasant experience for her. She did not like it at all. Not one bit. She couldn't keep up with her bills, including her Home Owners' Association (HOA) fees and common assessments.

She knew everyone in the building and they knew her. She had assumed that the Association, having known her for decades, would be a little flexible and patient. She was wrong. Someone once told her that one should never assume anything, because assumptions were almost always erroneous. In this case, there were a lot of owners who were defaulting on their fees and assessments. The Association began to place liens on these unit owners, including her. Then, she received a legal letter (as did the others), stating that foreclosure proceedings would soon be filed if the accounts were not brought current.

She knew that she needed to be brutally realistic and make some unpleasant choices, otherwise she would perish. So, she had no choice but to place her unit up for sale. The problem was that there were hundreds and hundreds of similar condos that were up for sale. It was a buyer's market.

Many speculators came through her unit, in the space of three months. She spent most of her time getting her place ready for viewings. She rejected low ball offer after low ball offer, until she realized that this was the best that she could get. She needed enough money (plus extra, to pay some outstanding creditors and have spare cash to live on) to buy a single family residential (detached) home which didn't have HOA fees. She accepted one low offer, which fell through at the last minute and then another, which also didn't work out. The third time was the charm. The price was obscenely low. She had a feeling that there would be a dry spell in the market, so she accepted the offer. If she hadn't, she would have lost her \$300,000.00 apartment – just because she owed \$4,900.00 and change in back HOA fees/assessments.

She moved quickly. Finding a home in a nice location, she scheduled the Closing date for her apartment sale and the purchase of her new home... in the same afternoon (three hours apart)! It was touch and go for awhile, but ultimately a success. She, however, was a wreck. Her stress level was so high that she felt sure that a blood vessel would soon burst in her eye. It happened whenever her blood pressure peaked at dangerously high levels. She tried a few breathing exercises, to calm herself down. "Chillax," she told herself. "The ordeal's over."

After the Closing, her realtor whispered to her that there was a tropical storm forecasted for later in the week and that, if the Closing hadn't happened when it did, there would have been a temporary moratorium on real estate Closings (in the region) because title companies prohibit the issuance of title insurance during severe storms.

"That was a close call," she thought to herself. Lady luck was on her side, after all.

She moved into her new home that night. Sitting on the hardwood floor in the living room, she felt so relieved. She opened a bottle of inexpensive champagne and poured herself a glass. Toasting to no one but herself, she sang out "L'Chaim!" (to Life!).

18/*Talking Him Off the Ledge*

He received the strangest voicemail message.

His friend's words were slow, yet they didn't quite make sense. He replayed the message three times. He called his friend back. No answer. Three hours later, his friend called again. He picked up the phone on the first ring. After the traditional niceties, there was a long pause. Then his friend said that she had been thinking about suicide because her life was a mess. His friend went on to say that there were serious financial worries, she couldn't focus on anything, her parents were not well, her father was acting erratically, and she had serious legal issues – but didn't want to elaborate. There was silence on the line. He talked to his friend for the next three hours. His friend listened.

He spoke to his friend a week later and was amazed at the 180° change in her. She had found a job, her legal issues were being sorted out and her father was receiving good medical treatment. He got off the phone and felt a surge of relief. His friend would be okay.

A few days later, the phone rang. The area code was the same, but not the number. He answered and on the other end was yet another friend of his. This friend was frantic and his speech was rapid and irrational. He knew that his friend wasn't under the influence of drugs or alcohol, but this particular fellow was prone to bouts of serious depression and melancholy. The friend, a brilliant and extremely well-educated man, was also out of work. Ageism was a factor in his inability to find a job. The other problem was that there was an air of despondency about the man, which was probably a bit off-putting to prospective employers. He talked to him, until he was certain that his friend had regained some sense of rationality. Over the next several weeks, they had many long telephone discussions.

And then, the phone calls stopped. He didn't hear from this particular friend for a long time. He was well aware that people sometimes go to extreme lengths when they think that there are no more options left. Worried, he left messages for him, but received no response. They lived states apart, and this made having person-to-person conversations difficult.

He hoped his friend was okay.

2011 – Enough, Already!

> *"When written in Chinese, the word "crisis" is composed of two characters – one represents danger and the other represents opportunity."*
>
> ~ John F. Kennedy, *12 April 1959*

In 2011, we heard economists bandying the term "double-dip recession" (still in denial – of the fact that the economic slump had indeed ***not*** ended in June 2009). In the words of Lakshman Achuthan, the Managing Director of ECRI (Economic Cycle Research Institute): "It's either just begun or it's right in front of us. But, at this point, that's a detail. The critical news is there's no turning back. We are going to have a new recession."[12]

As debt-ridden families continued to struggle under a weak labor market and low income levels, consumer spending was at an all-time low. In July 2011, the unemployment rate stood at 9.1% and more than 44% of the unemployed had been out of work (and steadily

[12] Chris Isidore,"Forecast says double-dip recession is imminent," *CNN Money,* September 30, 2011. http://money.cnn.com/2011/09/30/news/economy/double_dip_recession/index.htm (February 7, 2013).

looking for work) for over six months.[13] Long-term unemployment had become a serious problem, not to mention a demoralizing one.

Americans affected by the economic downturn were fed up. The question "*How soon will this be over?*" was replaced with "*Will this **ever** end?*"

With families living in a prolonged state of financial weakness, any unforeseen event (such as a serious medical problem, a death in the family, major car repair, or a lawsuit) could propel them into crisis mode, possible bankruptcy – or worse. And when this occurs, many find solace in their faith. CEO (Christmas and Easter Only) churchgoers suddenly start praying again. Praying hard. However, they're not necessarily praying at Church. With money being tight in so many middle-class households, dropping twenty dollars in a weekly collection basket may actually cause families some hardship. It is no surprise, therefore, that the practice of tithing (giving ten percent of one's income to a religious entity) is declining.

Practically speaking, as Pastor Keith Drury (Associate Professor of Religion at Indiana Wesleyan University) points out, "If your church has 100 working folk who give a percentage of their income to the church each month and 20% of them get laid off, they will tithe their unemployment check. When unemployment runs out

---

[13] U.S. Department of Labor, Bureau of Labor Statistics, *Current Population Survey* (Washington, DC: GPO, 2011).

and they have no income at all, they will tithe their income – but 10% of zero is zero."[14] Hence, the religious communities will have less money to support the outreach programs which, in turn, help people in need and so, unfortunately, the hardship propagates.

A few years back, there was a very fascinating (and spirited) scholarly debate in the press, on the subject of religiosity and the recession,[15] sparked by New York Times journalist Paul Vitello.[16] Vitello, using a 2007 article written by David Beckworth[17] (a Texas State University economics professor) to substantiate his argument that religious attendance rises exponentially during periods of economic crisis, got embroiled in an evidentiary kerfufel with pollster Frank Newport.[18] With Gallup® Poll stats at his fingertips, Newport

---

[14] Keith Drury, *"What will happen in the Church if we experience a deep recession (or mild depression),"* Website, October 7, 2008. http://www.drurywriting.com/keith/recession.depression.htm (February 10, 2013).

[15] Tobin Grant, "Recession and Religiosity Redux (Do evangelical churches see more members during a recession?)," *Christianity Today*, January 2, 2009. http://www.christianitytoday.com/ct/2009/januaryweb-only/153-51.0.html (February 10, 2013).

[16] Paul Vitello, "Bad Times Draw Bigger Crowds to Churches," *New York Times*, December 13, 2008. http://www.nytimes.com/2008/12/14/nyregion/14churches.html?_r=0 (February 10, 2013).

[17] David Beckworth, *"What Does the Recession Mean for Religiosity?"* Website, January 9, 2008. http://macromarketmusings.blogspot.com/2008/01/what-does-recession-mean-for.html (February 10, 2013).

[18] Frank Newport, "No Evidence Bad Times Are Boosting Church Attendance," *Gallup®*, December 17, 2008. http://www.gallup.com/poll/113452/Evidence-Bad-Times-Boosting-Church-Attendance.aspx (February 10, 2013).

refuted Vitello's article in a formal letter to the New York Times, claiming that the statistics clearly showed that church attendance remained steady (business as usual), despite the economic downturn. Adding fuel to the fire, *Slate* editor-at-large Jack Shafer quoted Newport's letter (and stats) in his own article, *Bogus Trend of the Week: Booming Evangelical Attendance.*[19] Shafer's sarcastic commentary subsequently annoyed Trinity College (Hartford, Connecticut) Professor of Religion in Public Life, Mark Silk, who publicized a retort, part of which is quoted below:

> "Unbeknownst to Shafer, however, is the bogosity of Gallup's church attendance numbers. What Newport doesn't say is that his company's surveys have shown church attendance to be in that exact numeric neighborhood ever since they began asking the question 60 years ago. As sure as death and taxes, two in five Americans will say they attend church weekly.
>
> But for over a decade, sociologists of religion (and those who read them) have known that 1) a lot of those supposed weekly attenders are fibbing; and 2) more of them are fibbing now than used to. The evidence for this comes from multiple sources, including time-usage studies, on-the-ground observation of parking lots, church attendance records, interviews with clergy."[20]

A fascinating argument, indeed. A Harvard-educated professor – specializing in the study of Religion in

---

[19] Jack Shafer, "Bogus Trend of the Week: Booming Evangelical Attendance," *Slate*, December 22, 2008. http://www.slate.com/articles/news_and_politics/press_box/2008/12/bogus_trend_of_the_week_booming_evangelical_attendance.html (February 10, 2013).

[20] Mark Silk, "Bogus Bogus Trend Story?" *Christianity Today,* December 23, 2008. http://blog.christianitytoday.com/ctpolitics/2008/12/bogus_bogus_tre.html (February 10, 2013).

America, Religion in Media and Intellectual History of the West – daring to refute statistics gathered by standardized polls and surveys, suggesting that the numbers may be stale and that they most definitely do not take into consideration certain socio-religious factors (such as people fibbing about their church attendance, for example) and direct (face-to-face) information that can only be gathered through on-the-ground research.

Does this sound familiar?

Yes, standard statistics are indeed very useful, but they are flawed. As Professor Silk stated, they are not completely accurate and, in my view, they should not be regarded as the Holy Grail for quantifying (with a stellar degree of accuracy) a state of mind, of being and – in the context of this book – the ***economy***. Or, more to the point, the millions of Americans who have been severely impacted by this economic crisis and who fall through the statistical cracks.

As to whether or not people attend – more frequently – their church, synagogue, mosque (or wherever we choose to go to find some Grace and solace) during times of severe economic hardship – well, I don't have a definitive answer, either way.

Faith is a very personal thing. For many, faith is what embraces us during our darkest moments. So, it is not inconceivable that we would gravitate to a place where we feel safe, in a haven that is free of harshness.

Whether we ascribe to a religious faith or not, there is one thing that we all could probably reach consensus on: Hope.

Hope comes to us in many guises. The important thing is that we recognize it when it does – whether it appears through the kindness of a stranger or in the necessity of having to go to "Plan B."

At least there *is* a Plan B. Actually, there's *always* a Plan B to be found, just as there is always hope.

19/Litigation Central

"Hello? Hello?" She heard someone call from outside, at the front of the gate. She looked through the window blinds in the sunroom. She saw a woman, dressed in business clothes, holding a clipboard in her hand. She couldn't discern whether it was a Jehovah's Witness devotee or a political canvasser, so she went outside to find out. She was wrong on both counts. The woman introduced herself as a court bailiff and very politely served her legal papers. Apparently, she was being sued. The woman, noting her shocked expression, spoke kindly to her and said that, if she couldn't afford a lawyer, that there were free legal aid services available. They exchanged polite goodbyes.

She went inside and poured herself a cup of tea. Her mother always used to say that a nice, strong cup of tea helps clear the mind. She read the Complaint. Essentially, several relatives (and their families) were involved in a series of joint business ventures. A few of the families were under considerable financial stress and one of them decided that the only option was to request the liquidation of all ventures and assets, without any regard for the wishes and finances of the other relatives (herself included). The request was denied since everyone would have incurred great financial loss, due to the dismal state of the economy. In a fit of rage, the family in question proceeded to launch an onslaught of lawsuits against everyone. Family should not sue family. Muttering to herself, she said, ***"Who does that?"***

She knew that hiring a good lawyer would be more than she could afford at the moment and perhaps a bit premature. She had twenty days in which to file a response, an "Answer." She spent the next nineteen days researching and learning all that she could on Civil Procedure. She prepared an Answer that was as professional as any lawyer could have done. She found out that she could file it via fax, without having to go to the courthouse. She filed it on the twentieth day.

A few weeks later, the FedEx truck stopped in front of her house. She went out and the driver asked her to sign for the envelope. She did. Inside the envelope were court papers from a jurisdiction outside the country. The Complaints, though different, were from the same people. Not strangers. No... much, much closer to home.

The lawsuits were personal, and personal lawsuits, by virtue of their emotional nature, can get nasty.

Which they did.

A few months later, the FedEx truck stopped in front of her house... again. She was not at all surprised that there was an envelope containing a third lawsuit.

They were using the legal system to carry out a personal vendetta. The expression "Don't let the bastards get you down" popped into her mind as she went about the business of educating herself on the legal process. When their lawyers started throwing multiple motions at her, she decided that it was time to retain a lawyer of her own.

Time is money. Acutely aware of this, she was very hands-on with her lawyers, so as to minimize the legal costs. However, she was not going to allow her financial vulnerability to be taken advantage of by predators.

In the end, the lawsuits fizzled. Each side wasted money. More importantly, relationships were severed beyond repair. A series of seemingly benign joint ventures, initially entered into with good intent by all parties, became a source of such contention that the complete destruction of family ties was inevitable. During hard economic times, litigation should not be employed as the first option for conflict resolution. The only people who really win are the lawyers. And, when it comes to personal lawsuits, well, vengeance reaps profit for them. The lawyers, that is. It's easy money in the bank.

"There are a lot of bullies and fear mongers out there," she thought to herself, as she archived her legal files. "The key thing to note is... don't be guided by fear, or you will perish."

20/*Faith, a Powerful Tonic*

They thought that attending the baptism of their friend's baby daughter would be a welcome and much-needed distraction. For one afternoon, they could put all their troubles aside and partake in a joyous and blessed occasion. In the last two years, life had been spiraling out of control. Food and money were scarce. They had lost their car. They had nearly lost their home. They needed something to grasp on to. They needed a little hope. And so, they thought that participating in a young child's first Sacrament would remind them of all things good – purity, innocence, new beginnings, Faith.

They gathered up what little cash they had ($58) to pay for the train and taxi that they would have to take. What would have taken them half an hour by car was going to be a three-hour transit ordeal (there was no public bus route in the area they were traveling to). They dressed up in their Sunday best and began their journey. When they got off the train, there were no taxis in sight. The afternoon heat and humidity made their clothes stick to their bodies. They realized that they may have to walk for at least an hour or so, if they didn't find a taxi. They would miss the Baptism. They began to walk and then spotted a cab parked nearby, hidden by a big tree. The driver was standing by the car. He was a *small, wiry man with dark, wrinkled skin, grey hair and white teeth. But it was his hazel eyes that caught their attention. Or, rather, what his eyes conveyed. Old eyes (although he didn't look more than 50) – eyes that had seen much and learned much. They had one of those déja-vu moments where they felt that they had met him before, that they knew him and he knew them. But, they hadn't. He asked them if he could drive them anywhere. They nodded and asked how much it would cost to get to their destination. The driver said "$48." They told him that they only had $38 left (not enough for the taxi fare and tip). They had spent $20 on two return train tickets and were hoping to get a lift back (from friends) to the train station, after the Baptism party. The driver looked at them kindly and said, $38 would be fine. They were elated and hopped into the air-conditioned cab.*

They exchanged pleasantries and names. The driver's name was Mohammed. He was from Pakistan and had come to America to make a better life for his siblings, wife and children. He hadn't always been a taxi driver. Like everyone else, he had been adversely affected by the economic downturn. He had worked long shifts to pay for his children's tuition. He had put his sister through medical school. Education, according to Mohammed, was the key to freedom and empowerment. They agreed. He went on to say that "Faith is what helps us to put one foot in front of the other and carry on, day after day, despite the troubles looming all around us." His eyes met theirs in the rearview mirror. Everyone was silent for the rest of the ride.

When they arrived at the church, Mohammed got out and opened the door for them. They shook his hand, thanked him, and once again apologized that they could only give him $38. He brushed their apologies aside and said "Enjoy your blessed event and the company of your friends. Leave your worries at the door." With that, he went into his car and drove away. Feeling uplifted, they smiled at each other and walked, hand-in-hand, into the church.

21/Plan B

He lost everything – well, almost everything.

His business – died an unceremonious death.
His home – repossessed by the bank.
His furnishings and household goods – marauded by creditors.
His cars – repossessed by the dealership.

Was there anything left?

He had his wife and child. Thankfully, they all had their health. Adversity had brought them even closer together.

And there was that small plot of land, in another state.

He had purchased the land for next to nothing in a tax sale, more than a decade earlier. Located in an idyllic (Thomas Kinkade-like) rural town, the five-acre plot had a forest of beautiful evergreens surrounding a graded area where there was a small shed, a well, and an old pick-up truck. He knew that this was where he and his family would begin a new and very different life. He asked a good friend of his for a big favor — to drive him and his family across a few state lines, to their little slice of heaven. He will always remember his friend's kindness as not only did he drive them there, but the dear man also brought along a supply of food, a small generator (and propane), spare gas for the truck, and some tools for them to use for as long as they needed them.

When they finally arrived, weary from the long road trip, they got out and stretched their legs. He laughed when he saw his daughter's mouth form into a wide "O" as she looked at the stunning scenery. He knew that she was thinking that it looked like an enchanted forest, straight out of one of her Hobbit stories. He also knew that she was aching to go and explore and so he promised her that they would do so, but only after they got themselves all settled in.

His wife unlocked the shed and immediately set about cleaning and organizing everything. It was not in good shape but it would have to do. They would have to live there until he built them a proper cottage-style home.

His friend was trying to get the old pick-up truck started. After about an hour, it actually sputtered to life! He and his friend high-fived each other.

It was starting to get a bit nippy, so they made a makeshift fire pit and started to burn some split logs. They roasted marshmallows and he smiled as he looked at his wife. She looked relaxed for the first time in two years. Her cheeks were getting rosy and she was smiling from ear to ear. God, he loved her smile!

He picked up a piece of spare wood. It was oak. He took his knife out of his jacket and started carving. He had almost forgotten what it felt like to work with wood. When he was younger, he used to do a lot of carpentry with his father. His father told him that he was really good at it, but he ended up choosing a different path.

Holding this wood in his hand... it felt right, somehow. Suddenly, he was overcome by a sense of lightness and freedom. It's a sensation that is often experienced when one gets to wipe the slate clean and the anticipation of beginning a fresh, new chapter becomes nothing short of exhilarating.

"It's funny how the things that we're passionate about when we're young, often end up being the things we revisit when we're older," he thought to himself.

Tomorrow, he would begin the first day in his new life – a carpenter. Why not? He had absolutely nothing to lose. He smiled to himself and his eyes were bright.

He joined his family and his good friend by the fire. They started to sing some camp songs. Somewhere in the distance, an owl hooted.

2012 – Is It Really Over?

> *"Federal Reserve Chairman Ben Bernanke said a failure to reach a deal for the fiscal cliff will hurt the recovery. The good news is most Americans will not be affected by this because they had no idea there WAS a recovery."*
>
> ~ Jay Leno

It has been said that many a true word is spoken in jest.

Long term unemployment can be like the kiss of death. The longer one remains unemployed, the less likely one is to actually get a job – because he/she becomes less marketable and therefore less desirable to a prospective employer. Additionally, the prolonged inactivity can be demotivating and may frequently cause one's skills to deteriorate.

By June 2012, 5.4 million Americans were unemployed for more than 27 weeks. At least 649,000 Americans have been unemployed for over three years.[21] About

[21] U.S. Department of Labor, Bureau of Labor Statistics, *Current Population Survey* (Washington, DC: GPO, 2012).

half of that number can be attributed to people who have been unemployed for four to five years. Most states provide unemployment insurance for 26 weeks. The federal government has provided additional assistance (for up to 99 weeks) for states that have been hit the hardest on the unemployment scale. However, for the severely long term unemployed, the assistance has expired.

A recovery? This feels more like a chronic illness.

Sporadic employment (contract or part-time work here and there) is often just enough to tide people over. Such temporary employees and consultants endure a higher personal risk of ruin, since they do not typically have health insurance or other benefits. Furthermore, they have the added instability/insecurity caused by not being able to predict if/when the next contract or job will come along. And, for workers who are over 55 and/or who are not in the best of health, the stress and uncertainty of sporadic employment could possibly cause them to degenerate – physically, as well as psychologically.

22/*My Truck, My Home*

He walked out of the post office and made his way towards his car, when he noticed a familiar truck parked in a nearby space. He peered through the window and recognized his friend – tousled grey hair, dressed in wrinkled clothes, with mouth agape, sleeping soundly while a laptop lay open on the passenger seat. He noticed the disarray of boxes and miscellaneous clothes on the back seat. Nearby, a church bell rang – startling his friend out of what appeared to be a much needed nap. When his friend noticed him, he rolled down his window and chuckled sheepishly.

He asked his friend how the contract work was going. His friend grimaced and said that things were sporadic, at best, and that he had felt compelled to take a rate cut because most companies were no longer paying the customary consultant fee. The fellow traveled wherever there was a gig, whether this meant going out of state ... or not. Not wanting to spend any income on hotels or motels, the poor man slept in his car.

His friend's wife was not in the best of health, which meant that being out of work was not an option. So, even if it meant being away for periods of time, then that's what he needed to do, to be able to provide for her healthcare.

He admired his friend's tenacity, but was worried about the man's lack of physical resilience. The week before, they were chatting on the phone and he realized his friend hadn't said a word for awhile. Then he heard his buddy snore. The guy had fallen asleep!

"That's a hard life," he thought to himself. He made some calls and referred his friend to some local contacts. Hopefully, the fellow would land some gigs closer to home.

2013 – Epilogue

"For we, the people, understand that our country cannot succeed when a shrinking few do very well and a growing many barely make it. We believe that America's prosperity must rest upon the broad shoulders of a rising middle class. We know that America thrives when every person can find independence and pride in their work; when the wages of honest labor liberate families from the brink of hardship."

~ President Barack Obama, excerpt from *2013 Inaugural Address*

The only way that America will thrive is if we – *individually and as a Nation* – stop over-spending and over-consuming and begin to live within our means.

The only way that America will thrive is if we – individually *and as a Nation* – make some tough decisions, regardless of whether or not they are popular decisions.

The only way that America will thrive is if our leaders – Commander-in-Chief, congressmen, congresswomen, Senators, Governors and Municipal Commissioners (to the Left and to the Right) – cooperate with each other and collaborate in a completely bipartisan effort to bring the American economy back from the abyss.

The only way that America will thrive is if our leaders make the economy their number one priority. Everything else trails from the economy.

We have not "bucked the recession."
We are not in danger of going into another recession.
We are there already.
We never left.
That is why it is a depression.

Individually, and as a Nation – let's lance this abscess, so that the stories that we hear will no longer be tales of hardship and despair, but of prosperity and pride.

23/*Coffee Shop Jive*

It took him only fifteen minutes to walk to the coffee shop. It was hot and humid, but he was used to it. The Panama hat that he wore shielded him from the sun, which was a good thing. He opened the door and was greeted by a blast of frosty air. "The staff always keeps the air conditioning on way too high," he muttered to himself. His favorite seat by the window was thankfully empty, so he strode over and placed his computer bag down.

Looking around, he noticed all the regulars. There were students, architects, retailers, some mellow reggae musicians, a poet and a few homeless veterans who had a lot of interesting stories to tell. Everyone usually stayed there for at least three or four hours, nursing their one cup of coffee and nibbling on a pastry. Money was still very tight for most people. The coffee shop was over-priced, but the customers enjoyed the music. The ambiance was nice.

He remarked to himself that he hadn't seen some of his old buddies and colleagues for a long, long time. 2013 sure looked and felt a hell of a lot different from 2006. A lifetime ago. Back then, they were all starting to feel the pinch of a tanking economy. One by one, his friends dropped out of the consulting scene. A few went bankrupt. Some divorced. Others had left the state and even the country. A few had died. There were several guys who seemed to have fallen off the face of the earth. He decided to check his LinkedIn, to see if they had made any status updates.

He fired up his computer and, after an annoying few minutes, was able to sign on to his LinkedIn. "The Wi-Fi is really slow in this coffee shop," he mumbled. He clicked on some of his connections and what he read made him throw his head back and laugh out loud. One of his engineering friends wrote, under "Current Job:" **... *"Something Entirely Different."***

As he scrolled down, he noticed that most of them were doing something entirely different. And he was no exception. That's the nature of the beast. When the economy tanks and stays tanked for such a long time, you either sink or swim. You hope for the best, but plan for the worst. It's called Plan B. The interesting thing is that sometimes "Plan B" turns out to be the best thing that ever happened to you.

He started moving his leg to the music. It was an old reggae song by Frighty & Colonel Mite. The title, "Life (Is What You Make It)."

(**PS:** Seriously, this was truly the actual song that was playing!)

Conclusions

> *"I am a firm believer in the people. If given the truth, they can be depended upon to meet any national crises. The great point is to bring them the real facts."*
>
> ~ Abraham Lincoln

My purpose for writing this book is threefold.

First, I wanted to share some real-life stories of people who are very new to the experience of joblessness, homelessness, and hunger. I wrote them not as short stories, but as vignettes which spotlight some of the most challenging (and, quite often, inspirational) moments in their lives – set in an eight-year time capsule that was and is one of the harshest economic downturns in recent history. These little "snapshots in words" are written in such a way so that you, the reader, can feel their hardship, appreciate their pain and understand their mindset.

They are all real stories of people who would die rather than be pitied. They just want their stories told, while maintaining their privacy and dignity. And, although I call them "Casualties" of the ~~Recession~~ Depression, because they have been so adversely affected by this very long economic downturn, they are – in fact – ***survivors***. This experience has taught them some very harsh life lessons and their faces show the signs of wear and tear. They are resilient and proud. They are the people who will rise again – to teach, invent, design, build, write, heal, and lead. And their hard-earned wisdom will likely benefit generations to come.

Second, I wanted to drive home the premise that the "Great Recession" (a label assigned by economists and political leaders) did not end in June 2009, but that it continues to this day (Q1 2013).

It appears that the statistics relied on by analysts do not take into account the severely long term unemployed (out of work for three years or more) – the men and women who (a) may have continued to seek work but have become less marketable to prospective employers and therefore less employable; and (b) may be so demoralized that they no longer have the energy or motivation to find work because they've given up hope. Furthermore, the statistics do not take into consideration the students who, after graduation, have been unable to find jobs. Sadly, this young demographic will be remembered in the history books as "Generation Jobless."

Another statistical omission is the problem of identifying and quantifying the families who are still living in their foreclosed homes – in some cases, for well over a year after a foreclosure judgment has been filed. The staggering amount of shadow inventory of bank-owned homes is unprecedented and managing all of it is most likely a challenging, perhaps even overwhelming, endeavor. And finally, the statistics do not take into consideration the middle-class hungry – Americans who don't have enough money to feed their families and who may be too proud and therefore unwilling to apply for social assistance (such as food stamps) from the state or local communities. These are the people who may be living with relatives or friends, hoping that the situation will be a temporary one.

It is apparent to me that these demographics have been overlooked when determining whether a recession has begun or ended, and at what point a recession becomes a depression. I contend that since economic activity has still not *"returned to close to normal levels"* (i.e. pre-December 2007), we are therefore ***not*** in recovery, ***not*** in a recession, ***not*** facing the possibility of a double-dip recession – we are in a depression. It is not a depression like the Great Depression of 1929-1939, but a depression nevertheless.

This brings me to my third and final reason for writing this book. It is encapsulated in President Lincoln's words, quoted at the beginning of this chapter and now, once again, for emphasis: *"I am a firm believer in the people. If given the truth, they can be depended upon to meet any national crises. The great point is to bring them the real facts."*

We, the people, are neither stupid nor gullible. We are intelligent enough to recognize that some statistics can be presented to the public, so as to project a positive, upbeat spin on things – while other statistics may be downplayed, so as to tell a different story. I believe that Americans can handle the truth, even if it may be disheartening. We are a strong nation, full of fighters. And, by nature, most of us are optimistic. This depression *will* pass and we will be prosperous once again.

There is a caveat, however. If we do not work together (people and leaders; the political left, right, and in-between), and if we do not cast our personal or political agendas aside, then we will be in this depression for the long haul.

It is not my intention to point fingers at any political leader or party. Nor am I interested in engaging in an ideological battle of red versus blue (or vice versa). I am, however, raising an eyebrow at the seemingly dismissive attitude that our politicians and economists have towards the ongoing severity of this economic "trough" and, by association, the degenerative effects on the country's largest demographic – the middle class. The bottom line is: if there are middle-class Americans who continue to experience economic hardship, then the problem *still* exists. If they are not in the process of recovering, then we are *not* "in a recovery."

It is the responsibility of our elected leaders to work together, on behalf of all the people (not just the few), to lift this country back on it's feet, to breathe some more life back into our technology epicenter – Silicon Valley, to ensure that people have the opportunity to work and prosper so that they may have food on their tables and a roof over their heads, and to help a hard working nation find a reason to get up in the morning.

— Heather Joan Marinos

Acknowledgements

It has been an honor and a privilege for me to tell these stories. Thank you to each of you (you know who you are) for allowing me to recount these deeply personal experiences. I hope I did them justice.

My apologies to those whose stories I did not tell. I could easily have filled up three tomes with all the material I had, but I thought that keeping them down to 23 vignettes would have more impact.

Thank you to those (again, you know who you are) who steered me through the editing process and gave me honest, critical feedback – not mincing any words. But, as you know, I like to keep it real.

A jubilant shout-out to my friends and some special members of my family (who live miles and oceans apart) for always cheering me on.

Finally, to the man who always calls me a "bleeding heart" but who really wouldn't have it any other way – not *for all the scotch in Scotland.* To him, I say *thank you, thank you, thank you.*

About the Author

"Experience is one thing you can't get for nothing"

~ Oscar Wilde

Born and raised in Montréal, Canada, Heather Joan Marinos has traveled extensively in Europe and resides permanently in the United States – in the wonderfully eclectic South Florida village called Coconut Grove.

A love of history and philosophy (especially the existentialists!) prompted her to do a B.A. (1981) in Political Science (specifically, political philosophy) and an M.A. (1988) in History (history of European intellectual thought) at McGill University and Concordia University, respectively.

A versatile writer famous for her love of good quotes, Heather has been writing for as long as she can remember. Her extensive writing and editing experience span a spectrum of markets – from high-tech, non-profit, history and politics to medical, travel, food and wine, and the performing arts. Added to the mix are 25+ years of well-honed strategic marketing and planning experience – both international and domestic.

Casualties of the ~~Recession~~ Depression is her first book, under her own name.

She is currently gathering research for a book on the new faces of the global recession, with a focus on Europe – more specifically, Greece.

Additionally, Heather has multiple book projects in different stages of development: a series of four non-fiction books targeted to the "Baby Boomer" generation and her first novel, *Finding Grace*.

She is an insomniac.

Bibliography

American Psychological Association. *APA Poll Finds Women Bear Brunt of Nation's Stress, Financial Downturn.* (October 7, 2008). Last Accessed February 6, 2013. http://www.apa.org/news/press/releases/2008/10/stress-women.aspx.

American Psychological Association. *Stress in America 2008.* (October 7, 2008). Last Accessed February 6, 2013. http://www.apa.org/news/press/releases/2008/10/stress-in-america.pdf.

Beckworth, David. "What Does the Recession Mean for Religiosity?" *Website.* (January 9, 2008). Last Accessed February 10, 2013. http://macromarketmusings.blogspot.com/2008/01/what-does-recession-mean-for.html.

Bureau of the Census. U.S. Department of Commerce, *Income, Poverty, and Health Insurance Coverage in the United States.* (Washington, DC: GPO, 2008-2012).

Bureau of Economic Analysis. U.S. Department of Commerce, *National Income and Product Accounts.* (Washington, DC: GPO, 2008-2012).

Bureau of Labor Statistics. U.S. Department of Labor, *Current Employment Statistics.* (Washington, DC: GPO, 2008-2012).

Bureau of Labor Statistics. U.S. Department of Labor, *Current Population Survey.* (Washington, DC: GPO, 2008-2012).

Bureau of Labor Statistics. U.S. Department of Labor, The Editor's Desk, *Increase in unemployment rate in January 2009.* Last Accessed February 6, 2013. http://www.bls.gov/opub/ted/2009/feb/wk2/art02.htm.

Burgard, Sarah. "Mental Health and the Great Recession." *2012 Health,* Stanford Center on Poverty and Inequality. Stanford, CA: 2012.

Drury, Keith. "What will happen in the Church if we experience a deep recession (or mild depression)," *Website.* (October 7, 2008). Last Accessed February 10, 2013. http://www.drurywriting.com/keith/recession.depression.htm.

Feeding America. *Top 10 Facts About Millions of Americans Living on the Brink of Hunger.* Chicago, Illinois: December 18, 2012. Last Accessed February 6, 2013. http://feedingamerica.org/press-room/press-releases/top-ten-facts-about-millions-of-americans-living-on-the-brink-of-hunger.aspx.

Grant, Tobin. "Recession and Religiosity Redux (Do evangelical churches see more members during a recession?)," *Christianity Today*, January 2, 2009. Last Accessed February 10, 2013. http://www.christianitytoday.com/ct/2009/january web-only/153-51.0.html.

Isidore, Chris. "Forecast says double-dip recession is imminent," *CNN Money* (September 30, 2011). Last Accessed February 7, 2013. http://money.cnn.com/2011/09/30/news/economy/double_dip_recession/index.htm.

National Bureau of Economic Research (NBER). *The NBER's Business Cycle Dating Committee*. Last Accessed January 29, 2013. http://www.nber.org/cycles/recessions.html.

National Coalition for the Homeless et al. *Foreclosure to Homelessness 2009: the forgotten victims of the subprime crisis* (2009): 14. Last Accessed February 6, 2013. http://www.nationalhomeless.org/advocacy/ForeclosuretoHomelessness0609.pdf.

Newport, Frank. "No Evidence Bad Times Are Boosting Church Attendance," *Gallup*®, December 17, 2008. Last Accessed February 10, 2013. http://www.gallup.com/poll/113452/Evidence-Bad-Times-Boosting-Church-Attendance.aspx.

RealtyTrac®. *U.S. Foreclosure Market Report*™ *for Q3 2009*. (October 15, 2009). Last Accessed February 6, 2013. http://www.realtytrac.com/foreclosure/foreclosure-rates.html.

RealtyTrac®. *2012 Year-end Metro Foreclosure Market Report*™. (January 28, 2013). Last Accessed February 6, 2013. http://www.realtytrac.com/content/foreclosure-market- report/2012-metro-foreclosure-report-7575.

Shafer, Jack . "Bogus Trend of the Week: Booming Evangelical Attendance," *Slate*, December 22, 2008. Last Accessed February 10, 2013. http://www.slate.com/articles/news_and_politics/press_box/2008/12/bogus_trend_of_the_week_booming_evangelical_attendance.html.

Silicon Valley Leadership Group. *2007 Silicon Valley Projections (Tough Challenges- Hopeful Signs).* Last Accessed February 4, 2013. http://svlg.org/wpcontent/uploads/2011/04/projections_2007.pdf.

Silk, Mark. "Bogus Bogus Trend Story?" *Christianity Today*, December 23, 2008. Last Accessed February 10, 2013. http://blog.christianitytoday.com/ctpolitics/2008/12/bogus_bogus_tre.html.

Smith, Adam. *Wealth of Nations*, edited by C. J. Bullock. Vol. X. The Harvard Classics. New York: P.F. Collier & Son, 1909–14; Bartleby.com, 2001.

Steinhauer, Jennifer. "Coffers Empty, California Pays With IOUs," *New York Times*, July 3, 2009.

U.S. Conference of Mayors. *Hunger and Homelessness Survey: A Status Report on Hunger and Homelessness in America's Cities,* December 2011. Last Accessed February 6, 2012. http://usmayors.org/pressreleases/uploads/2011-hhreport.pdf.

U.S. Department of Agriculture. Supplemental Nutrition Assistance Program, *SNAP Monthly Data.* (Washington, DC: GPO, February 8, 2013).

U.S. Department of Housing and Urban Development. 2012 HUD report on *Homeless Populations and Subpopulations*. Last Accessed February 9, 2013. http://www.hudhre.info/CoC_Reports/2012_national_pops_sub_FULL.pdf.

Vitello, Paul. "Bad Times Draw Bigger Crowds to Churches," *New York Times*, December 13, 2008. Last Accessed February 10, 2013. http://www.nytimes.com/2008/12/14/nyregion/14churches.html?_r=0.

Weller, Christian E. *The U.S. Economy in Review: 2006,* Center for American Progress. (December 21, 2006). Last Accessed January 29, 2013. http://www.americanprogress.org/issues/economy/news/2006/12/21/2420/the-u-s-economy-in-review-2006/.

Appendix A – Statistics

As mentioned earlier in the Conclusions section of this book, the statistics provided by the U.S. Department of Labor's Bureau of Labor Statistics and the U.S. Census Bureau, though unarguably very detailed and comprehensive, do not take specific factors into account – such as the severely longterm (3 years$^+$) unemployed and some of the extenuating circumstances for their unemployment (although the statistics do cite some of the reasons). As well, the unreported families living in poverty (i.e. those who refuse to apply for social assistance) are not (and by their omission, *cannot*) be accounted for.

UNEMPLOYMENT

Here are some recent numbers from the Bureau of Labor Statistics, as of January 2013:

[**SOURCE:** U.S. Department of Labor, Bureau of Labor Statistics, *Website/Home Page*, Last Accessed February 9, 2013, from http://www.bls.gov/home.htm]

Household Data Annual Averages

Employment Status — *1997*-2012 Comparative Data

HOUSEHOLD DATA
ANNUAL AVERAGES
1. Employment status of the civilian noninstitutional population, 1942 to date — Continued
[Numbers in thousands]

Year	Civilian noninstitutional population	Civilian labor force								Not in labor force
		Total	Percent of population	Employed				Unemployed		
				Total	Percent of population	Agriculture	Nonagricultural industries	Number	Percent of labor force	
1997	203,133	136,297	67.1	129,558	63.8	3,399	126,159	6,739	4.9	66,837
1998	205,220	137,673	67.1	131,463	64.1	3,378	128,085	6,210	4.5	67,547
1999	207,753	139,368	67.1	133,488	64.3	3,281	130,207	5,880	4.2	68,385
2000	212,577	142,583	67.1	136,891	64.4	2,464	134,427	5,692	4.0	69,994
2001	215,092	143,734	66.8	136,933	63.7	2,299	134,635	6,801	4.7	71,359
2002	217,570	144,863	66.6	136,485	62.7	2,311	134,174	8,378	5.8	72,707
2003	221,168	146,510	66.2	137,736	62.3	2,275	135,461	8,774	6.0	74,658
2004	223,357	147,401	66.0	139,252	62.3	2,232	137,020	8,149	5.5	75,956
2005	226,082	149,320	66.0	141,730	62.7	2,197	139,532	7,591	5.1	76,762
2006	228,815	151,428	66.2	144,427	63.1	2,206	142,221	7,001	4.6	77,387
2007	231,867	153,124	66.0	146,047	63.0	2,095	143,952	7,078	4.6	78,743
2008	233,788	154,287	66.0	145,362	62.2	2,168	143,194	8,924	5.8	79,501
2009	235,801	154,142	65.4	139,877	59.3	2,103	137,775	14,265	9.3	81,659
2010	237,830	153,889	64.7	139,064	58.5	2,206	136,858	14,825	9.6	83,941
2011	239,618	153,617	64.1	139,869	58.4	2,254	137,615	13,747	8.9	86,001
2012	243,284	154,975	63.7	142,469	58.6	2,186	140,283	12,506	8.1	88,310

NOTE: Revisions to population controls and other changes can affect the comparability of labor force levels over time. In recent years, for example, updated population controls have been introduced annually with the release of January data. Information about historical comparability is online at www.bls.gov/cps/documentation.htm#comp.

[**SOURCE:** U.S. Department of Labor, Bureau of Labor Statistics, *Current Population Survey*, Last Accessed February 9, 2013, from http://www.bls.gov/cps/cpsaat01.pdf]

Household Data Annual Averages

Unemployed Persons (2012) — by reason for unemployment, sex*, age and duration of unemployment (* *the data by sex is not included here)*

HOUSEHOLD DATA
ANNUAL AVERAGES
29. Unemployed persons by reason for unemployment, sex, age, and duration of unemployment
[Percent distribution]

Reason, sex, and age	2012						
	Total unemployed		Duration of unemployment				
					15 weeks and over		
	Thousands of persons	Percent	Less than 5 weeks	5 to 14 weeks	Total	15 to 26 weeks	27 weeks and over
Total, 16 years and over	12,506	100.0	21.1	22.9	55.9	14.9	41.1
Job losers and persons who completed temporary jobs	6,877	100.0	21.7	22.1	56.2	14.5	41.7
On temporary layoff	1,183	100.0	50.7	30.5	18.8	11.7	7.2
Not on temporary layoff	5,694	100.0	15.7	20.3	64.0	15.1	48.9
Permanent job losers	4,447	100.0	13.3	19.1	67.6	15.2	52.4
Persons who completed temporary jobs	1,247	100.0	24.2	24.8	51.0	14.7	36.3
Job leavers	967	100.0	24.0	26.2	49.7	16.1	33.6
Reentrants	3,345	100.0	18.5	22.5	59.0	14.8	44.2
New entrants	1,316	100.0	22.9	25.9	51.2	15.9	35.3

[**SOURCE:** U.S. Department of Labor, Bureau of Labor Statistics, *Current Population Survey*, Last Accessed February 9, 2013, from http://www.bls.gov/cps/cpsaat29.htm]

Household Data Annual Averages

Persons Not in the Labor Force (2011-2012) — by desire and availability for work, age, and sex

HOUSEHOLD DATA
ANNUAL AVERAGES
35. Persons not in the labor force by desire and availability for work, age, and sex
[In thousands]

Category	Total		Age						Sex			
			16 to 24 years		25 to 54 years		55 years and over		Men		Women	
	2011	2012	2011	2012	2011	2012	2011	2012	2011	2012	2011	2012
Total not in the labor force	86,001	88,310	17,201	17,499	22,961	23,061	45,839	47,750	34,343	35,017	51,658	53,293
Do not want a job now(1)	79,564	81,752	15,177	15,383	20,107	20,248	44,280	46,120	31,298	31,989	48,266	49,763
Want a job(1)	6,437	6,558	2,023	2,115	2,854	2,813	1,560	1,630	3,045	3,028	3,392	3,530
Did not search for work in previous year	3,268	3,390	1,010	1,064	1,303	1,328	955	998	1,463	1,490	1,804	1,900
Searched for work in previous year, but not in past 4 weeks(2)	3,169	3,168	1,014	1,052	1,551	1,484	605	632	1,582	1,537	1,587	1,630
Not available to work now	597	651	262	282	262	288	73	82	236	253	361	399
Marginally attached (available to work now)(3)	2,573	2,516	752	770	1,289	1,196	532	550	1,346	1,285	1,227	1,232
Discouraged over job prospects(4)	989	909	222	217	519	451	248	241	579	541	410	368
Reasons other than discouragement	1,584	1,608	530	553	770	746	284	309	767	743	817	864
Family responsibilities	215	229	30	33	139	147	45	49	48	61	166	168
In school or training	323	339	245	257	75	73	4	9	183	175	140	164
Ill health or disability	169	168	18	18	93	83	58	66	86	80	83	87
Other(5)	877	871	238	245	463	442	177	185	449	427	428	444

Footnotes
(1) Includes some persons who are not asked if they want a job.
(2) Persons who had a job in the prior 12 months must have searched since the end of that job.
(3) Persons "marginally attached to the labor force" are those who want a job, have searched for work during the prior 12 months, and were available to take a job during the reference week, but had not looked for work in the past 4 weeks.
(4) Discouraged workers are persons marginally attached to the labor force who did not actively look for work in the prior 4 weeks for reasons such as thinks no work available, could not find work, lacks schooling or training, employer thinks too young or old, and other types of discrimination.
(5) Includes those who did not actively look for work in the prior 4 weeks for such reasons as child-care and transportation problems, as well as a small number for which reason for nonparticipation was not ascertained.

[**SOURCE:** U.S. Department of Labor, Bureau of Labor Statistics, *Current Population Survey*, Last Accessed February 9, 2013, from http://www.bls.gov/cps/cpsaat35.htm]

FORECLOSURES

According to RealtyTrac®, a leading supplier of real estate data in the United States, there were 1.8M (1,836,634) foreclosure filings in 2012. This included default notices, scheduled auctions and bank repossessions.

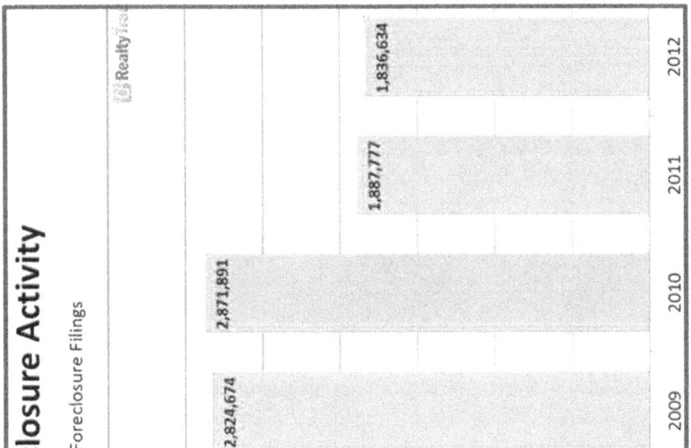

[**SOURCES:** RealtyTrac®. *2012 Year-end Foreclosure Market Report*™ (January 14, 2013), Last Accessed February 9, 2013, from http://www.realtytrac.com/Content/foreclosure-market-report/2012-year-end-foreclosure-market-report-7547]

Although the number of foreclosure filings has decreased somewhat since 2012, the numbers are still outrageously high.

According to RealtyTrac®, although U.S. foreclosures peaked at an all-time high in 2010, the number of foreclosures in 120 (of 212) nationwide metropolitan locations (with a population of 200,000+) ***increased*** in 2012 (from 2011) by **57%.**

Eight of the nation's 20 leading metro areas showed the most increased foreclosure activity in 2012, led by Tampa (↑80%), Miami (↑36%), Baltimore (↑34%), Chicago (↑30%), and New York (↑28%).

[**SOURCES:** RealtyTrac®. *2012 Year-end Metro Foreclosure Market Report™* (January 28, 2013), Last Accessed February 9, 2013, from http://www.realtytrac.com/content/foreclosure-market-report/2012-metro-foreclosure-report-7575]

HOMELESSNESS

Below is an excerpt from the U.S. Conference of Mayors' December 2012 report on *Hunger and Homelessness in America's Cities (a 25-city Survey).* It was found that – over the past year:

- *"The total number of persons experiencing homelessness increased across the survey cities by an average of 7%, with 60% of the cities reporting an increase..."*

- *"The number of families experiencing homelessness increased across the survey cities by an average of 8%, with 71% of the cities reporting an increase..."*

- *"The number of unaccompanied individuals experiencing homelessness over the past year increased across the survey cities by an average of 5%, with 35% reporting an increase..."*

- *"City officials cited the lack of affordable housing as the leading cause of homelessness among families with children. This was followed by poverty, unemployment, eviction, and domestic violence..."*

- *"Lack of affordable housing also led the list of causes of homelessness among unaccompanied individuals, followed by unemployment, poverty, mental illness and the lack of needed services, and substance abuse ..."*

- *"Officials in 60% of the survey cities expect the number of homeless families to increase over the next year..."*

- *"Officials in 56% of the cities expect the number of homeless unaccompanied individuals to increase over the next year."*

The 25 cities surveyed:

1. Asheville (NC)
2. Boston (MA)
3. Charleston (SC)
4. Charlotte (NC)
5. Chicago (IL)
6. Cleveland (OH)
7. Dallas (TX)
8. Denver (CO)
9. Des Moines (IA)
10. Gastonia (NC)
11. Los Angeles (CA)
12. Louisville (KY)
13. Minneapolis (MN)
14. Nashville (TN)
15. Norfolk (VA)
16. Philadelphia (PA)
17. Phoenix (AZ)
18. Portland (OR)
19. Providence (RI)
20. Saint Paul (MN)
21. Salt Lake City (UT)
22. San Antonio (TX)
23. San Francisco (CA)
24. Trenton (NJ)
25. Washington (DC)

[**SOURCE:** U.S. Conference of Mayors, *Hunger and Homelessness Survey: A Status Report on Hunger and Homelessness in America's Cities,* December 2011, p.2., Last Accessed February 9, 2013, from http://usmayors.org/pressreleases/uploads/2011-hhreport.pdf]

The 2012 HUD report on *Homeless Populations and Subpopulations,* (U.S. Department of Housing and Urban Development), the statistics provided by the CoC (Continuum of Care – a set of 3 competitively–awarded programs created to address the problems of homelessness in a comprehensive manner, with other federal agencies) presents these statistics **(they have not been independently verified)**:

Full Summary Report (All States, Territories, Puerto Rico and District of Columbia)

Summary by household type, aggregated:

	Sheltered			
	Emergency Shelter	Transitional Housing*	Unsheltered	Total
Households without children[1]	117,506	73,265	178,721	369,492
Households with at least one adult and one child[2]	32,605	29,191	15,361	77,157
Households with only children[3]	1,821	985	4,067	6,873
Total Homeless Households	**151,932**	**103,441**	**198,149**	**453,522**

	Sheltered			
	Emergency Shelter	Transitional Housing*	Unsheltered	Total
Persons in households without children[1]	121,408	74,529	190,667	386,604
Persons in households with at least one adult and one child[2]	101,218	89,778	48,407	239,403
Persons in households with only children[3]	1,973	1,249	4,553	7,775
Total Homeless Persons	**224,599**	**165,556**	**243,627**	**633,782**

Summary of homeless persons by subpopulations reported, aggregated:

	Sheltered	Unsheltered	Total
Chronically Homeless	32,647	67,247	99,894
Severely Mentally Ill	65,443	46,550	111,993
Chronic Substance Abuse	75,581	55,782	131,363
Veterans	35,143	27,476	62,619
Persons with HIV/AIDS	8,300	3,422	11,722
Victims of Domestic Violence	54,142	20,148	74,290
Unaccompanied Youth (Under 18)	2,746	3,886	6,632

* Safe Haven programs are included in the Transitional Housing category.
[1]This category includes single adults, adult couples with no children, and groups of adults.
[2]This category includes households with one adult and at least one child under age 18.
[3]This category includes persons under age 18, including children in one-child households, adolescent parents and their children, adolescent siblings, or other household configurations composed only of children.

Thursday, November 15, 2012

[**SOURCE:** U.S. Department of Housing and Urban Development, 2012 HUD report on *Homeless Populations and Subpopulations*, Last retrieved on February 9, 2013, from http://www.hudhre.info/CoC_Reports/2012_national_pops_sub_FULL.pdf]

POVERTY

Number in Poverty and Poverty Rates
1959-2011

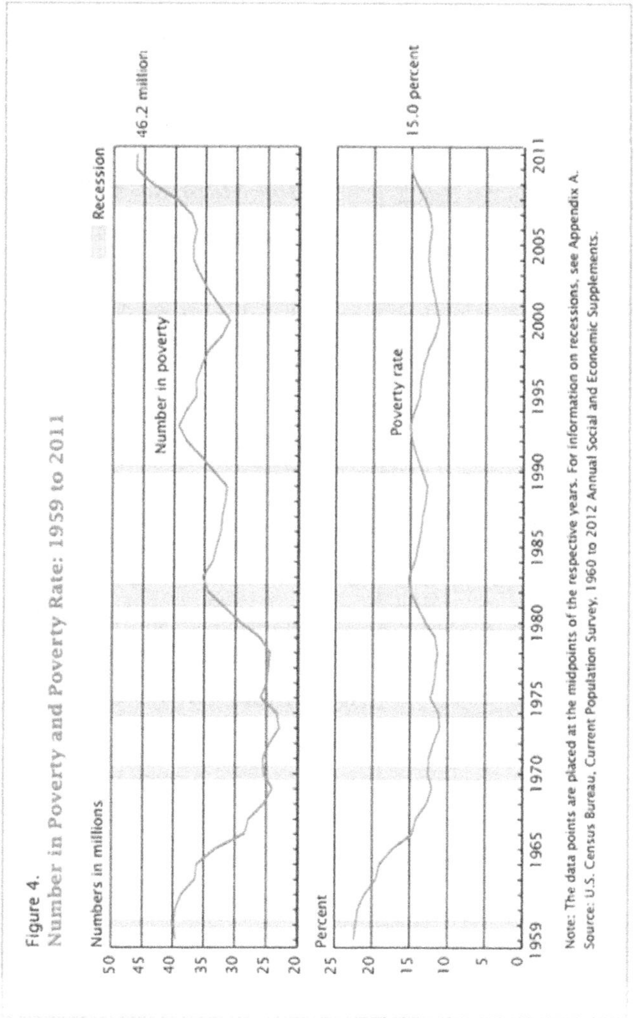

[**SOURCE:** U.S. Department of Commerce, U.S. Census Bureau, Last Accessed February 9, 2013, from http://www.census.gov/hhes/www/poverty/data/incpovhlth/2011/figure4.pdf]

HUNGER

SUPPLEMENTAL NUTRITION ASSISTANCE PROGRAM					
(Data, as of February 8, 2013)					
Fiscal	PARTICIPATION		BENEFIT	AVERAGE MONTHLY BENEFIT	
Year	Persons	Households	COSTS	Per Person	Per Household
ANNUAL SUMMARY					
FY 2013	47,622,363	22,980,792	12,815,483,317	134.55	278.83
FY 2012	46,609,072	22,329,713	74,619,830,164	133.41	278.48
FY 2011	44,708,726	21,072,113	71,810,924,022	133.85	283.99

Supplemental Nutrition Assistance Program (SNAP) – formerly known as ***Food Stamps*** – is the first "lifesaver" for the millions of Americans who are "food insecure" or downright starving.

As with all programs of this kind, SNAP is not immune to budget cuts. However – given this prolonged economic slump that we've been experiencing since December 2007 – cuts would be disastrous to millions of Americans for whom this program is their lifeline.

According to Feeding America (one of the nation's leading domestic hunger-relief charities, whose network of members supply food to more than 37 million Americans each year):

- 1 in 5 children lives in food insecure households
- 1 in 6 Americans is food insecure
- 1 in 7 Americans is enrolled in the Food Stamp program
- Nearly half of all SNAP participants are children

[**SOURCES:** U.S. Department of Agriculture. Supplemental Nutrition Assistance Program, *SNAP Monthly Data.* (February 8, 2013), Last Accessed February 9, 2013, from http://www.fns.usda.gov/pd/34SNAPmonthly.htm ***AND*** Feeding America. *Top 10 Facts About Millions of Americans Living on the Brink of Hunger.* Chicago, Illinois, December 18, 2012, Last Accessed February 9, 2013, from http://feedingamerica.org/press-room/press-releases/top-ten-facts-about-millions-of-americans-living-on-the-brink-of-hunger.aspx]

Another word on **HUNGER**:

Hunger is not a game. Right now, here in America, one in seven Americans is on food stamps. ***One in seven.*** The hungry (and the homeless) are not all derelicts and junkies. Many are middle-class families who were living from paycheck-to-paycheck, but then the paychecks suddenly stopped. They are homeowners, some of whom are now living in tents or tunnels – because banks have foreclosed on them and they have run out of options. They are men and women with medical bills so astronomically high that they have been forced into bankruptcy. They are young university students with $100,000$^+$ in student loans, who can't find jobs when they graduate – forced to begin their adult life with a huge debt load. They are professionals, with degrees and experience, who can't make ends meet.

We are not a third world country. We are a world super power and yet somehow a large portion of our population is hungry or, to use the politically correct term – *"food insecure."* This is simply not acceptable, certainly not in 2013.

As a nation, we pride ourselves on our strong sense of community. So, look to the right of you, and to the left. The person you see beside you may be someone who is hungry. Don't assume that because she is holding a designer handbag, that she is healthy and well-fed. For all you know, she may have bought that purse ten years ago, when times were better. Look beyond appearances and see, *really see*. Cast your judgments aside. Then, exercise your sense of community and extend a helping hand.

— **HJM**

Appendix B – Helpful Resources and Philanthropic Opportunities

Just as the serious problem of a depressed economy must be addressed and resolved in a collaborative, bi-partisan effort by our political leaders, so should we – the people – take the initiative to lend a helping hand to members of our community who are in need. Whether it be through random acts of kindness, volunteer work, advocacy support or financial contributions – it will at least be a way for us to be part of the process of recovery. Let the political leaders do what they know they need to do. And we will do our part.

Kindness is fulfilling.

The people we help will eventually recover and, when they do, the kindness they received will not likely be forgotten. And they will pay it forward. Thus, the cycle of kindness will continue.

The following pages provide a list of organizations, programs and helpful reading material that may be useful – both for those who are seeking assistance, information, legal advocacy or, simply advice, as well as for those who may want to engage in a little philanthropy – to make a positive difference in the community.

The resources listed here are merely the result of the author's research, which she is sharing with you, the reader. Each of the organizations' descriptions is listed from/on their respective websites.

It should be noted that the author of this book is not affiliated with any of these organizations, in any manner whatsoever, nor is she endorsing any specific organization.

ADVOCACY

The National Law Center on Homelessness & Poverty (NLCHP)

is committed to solutions that address the causes of homelessness, not just the symptoms, and works to place and address homelessness in the larger context of poverty. To this end, we employ three main strategies: impact litigation, policy advocacy, and public education. We are a persistent voice on behalf of homeless Americans, speaking effectively to federal, state, and local policy makers. We also produce investigative reports and provide legal and policy support to local organizations. You are invited to join the network of attorneys, advocates, students, activists, and committed individuals who support the Law Center. Our network provides a forum for individuals, non-profits, and corporations to participate and learn more about using the law to advocate for solutions to homelessness.

Website:
http://www.nlchp.org/
Contact Details:
1411 K Street NW, Suite 1400
Washington, DC 20005
Phone: (202) 638-2535
Informative Publication:
Eviction (Without) Notice: Renters and the Foreclosure Crisis (December 2012), can be retrieved from:
http://www.nlchp.org/content/pubs/Eviction_Without_Notice1.pdf

Philanthropy:
To Join
http://www.nlchp.org/join_us.cfm
To Donate
https://npo1.networkforgood.org/Donate/Donate.aspx?npoSubscriptionId=1005887&uniqueID=634810793557568713

CREDIT COUNSELING

National Foundation for Credit Counseling (NFCC) is one of the nation's largest financial counseling organization. The NFCC Member Agency Network includes more than 700 community-based offices located in all 50 states and Puerto Rico. More than 3 million consumers annually receive financial counseling and education from NFCC Member Agencies in person, over the phone, or online.

Website:
http://www.nfcc.org/
Contact Details:
2000 M Street NW, Suite 505
Washington, DC 20036
Phone: (202) 677-4300
or toll-free, at 1-800-388-2227

HOMELESSNESS/HOUSING ISSUES

National Alliance to End Homelessness (NAEH) is a non-profit, non-partisan organization committed to preventing and ending homelessness in the United States. The Alliance works to prevent and end homelessness in the following ways: working collaboratively with public, private, and nonprofit partners to develop, analyze and advocate for policy solutions; providing communities with best practices, how-to kits and technical assistance trainings that help communities implement solutions developed through policy, research and practice; and by advancing data and research so that policymakers, practitioners, and the public have the best information possible about trends in homelessness and emerging solutions.

Website:
www.naeh.org
Contact Details:
1518 K Street NW, Suite 410
Washington, DC 20005
Phone: (202) 638-1526
Philanthropy:
To Help
http://www.endhomelessness.org/pages/what_you_can_do
To Donate
http://www.endhomelessness.org/pages/donate1

The National Association for the Education of Homeless Children and Youth (NAEHCY)
is a national grassroots membership association, serves as the voice and the social conscience for the education of children and youth in homeless situations. NAEHCY connects educators, parents, advocates, researchers and service providers to ensure school enrollment and attendance in support of overall success for children and youth whose lives have been disrupted by the lack of safe, permanent, and adequate housing. NAEHCY accomplishes these goals through advocacy, partnerships and education.

Website:
www.naehcy.org.
Contact Details:
P.O. Box 26274
Minneapolis, MN 55426
Phone: (866) 862-2562
Philanthropy:
Get Involved
http://www.naehcy.org./about-naehcy/get-involved
To Join
http://www.naehcy.org./about-naehcy/become-a-member
To Donate
http://www.naehcy.org./donate

National Coalition for the Homeless (NCH) is a national network of people who are experiencing or have experienced homelessness, as well as activists, advocates, community-based and faith-based service providers and others committed to the single mission of ending homelessness through systemic and attitudinal change. The NCH also works to meet the immediate needs of people experiencing homelessness or who are at high risk of homelessness. NCH takes as its first principle that people who have experienced homelessness firsthand must be actively involved at all levels of its work. Toward this end, the NCH engages in public education, policy advocacy, and grassroots organizing, focusing on four areas: housing justice, economic justice, health care justice and civil rights.

Website:
www.nationalhomeless.org
Contact Details:
2201 P Street NW
Washington, DC 20037-1033
Phone: (202) 462-4822
Need Help?
*http://www.nationalhomeless.org/need_help/index.*html
Philanthropy:
To Help
http://www.nationalhomeless.org/want_to_help/index.html
To Join
http://www.nationalhomeless.org/about_us/membership.html
To Donate
http://www.nationalhomeless.org/donate/index.html

National Health Care for the Homeless Council (NHCHC)
is a membership organization engaged in research, education, training, advocacy and peer support. The Council began in 1984 as part of the 19-project HCH demonstration program of the Robert Wood Johnson Foundation and the Pew Memorial Trust. The Council now includes more than 1,000 individual and 100 organizational members who provide care for homeless persons or have themselves experienced homelessness. The Council's mission is to help bring about reform of the health care system to best serve the needs of people who are homeless, to work in alliance with others whose broader purpose is to eliminate homelessness and to provide support to Council members.

Website:
www.nhchc.org
Contact Details:
604 Gallatin Avenue, Suite 106
Nashville TN 37206
Phone: (615) 226-2292
Philanthropy:
To Join
https://www.nhchc.org/join/
To Donate
https://www.nhchc.org/donate/

National Low Income Housing Coalition (NLIHC) is dedicated to achieving socially just public policy assuring that people with the lowest incomes in the United States have affordable and decent homes. Our goals are to preserve existing federally-assisted homes and housing resources, expand the supply of low income housing, and establish housing stability as the primary purpose of federal low income housing policy.

Website:
www.nlihc.org
Contact Details:
712 15th Street NW, 6th Floor
Washington, DC 20005
Phone: (202) 662-1530
Philanthropy:
Get Involved
http://nlihc.org/involvement
To Join
http://nlihc.org/membership
To Donate
http://nlihc.org/donate

United States Department of Housing and Urban Development (HUD)

is working to strengthen the housing market to bolster the economy and protect consumers; meet the need for quality affordable rental homes: utilize housing as a platform for improving quality of life; build inclusive and sustainable communities free from discrimination; and transform the way HUD does business. HUD's mission is to create strong, sustainable, inclusive communities and quality affordable homes for all.

Website:
http://portal.hud.gov/hudportal/HUD
Contact Details:
451 7th Street S.W.
Washington, DC 20410
Phone: (202) 708-1112
Need Help?/Homeowners -
http://portal.hud.gov/hudportal/HUD?src=/homeownerhelp
Need Help?/Homeless -
http://portal.hud.gov/hudportal/HUD?src=/program_offices/comm_planning/homeless
Philanthropy:
Donate/Volunteer
http://www.usa.gov/Topics/Weather/Hurricane/sandy.shtml#Donate_and_Volunteer

United States Interagency Council on Homelessness (USICH)

is an independent agency within the federal executive branch. The mission of the United States Interagency Council on Homelessness (USICH) is to coordinate the federal response to homelessness and to create a national partnership at every level of government and with the private sector to reduce and end homelessness in the nation while maximizing the effectiveness of the Federal Government in contributing to the end of homelessness.

Website:
http://www.usich.gov/
Contact Details:
Federal Center SW, 409 3rd Street SW, Suite 310
Washington, DC 20024
Phone: (202) 708-4663
Informative Publication:
Opening Doors — Federal Strategy Plan to Prevent and End Homelessness, 2010
http://www.epaperflip.com/aglaia/viewer.aspx?docid=1dc1e97f82884912a8932a3502c37c02
Programs
http://www.usich.gov/funding_programs/programs/
Philanthropy:
Take Action
http://www.usich.gov/action/
Get Involved
http://www.usich.gov/action/individuals/
To Join
http://www.usich.gov/action/opening_doors_across_america/join_us_now_contact_us/

HUNGER

Feeding America

is a non-profit organization whose mission is to feed America's hungry through a nationwide network of member food banks and engage our country in the fight to end hunger. The values which guide all of our actions and planning are: Respect, Stewardship and Accountability, Collaboration, Urgency, Service, Integrity, and Diversity.

Website:
http://feedingamerica.org/
Contact Details:
35 East Wicker Drive, Suite 2000
Chicago, IL 60601
Phone: 1-800-771-2303
Informative Publication:
Hunger in America - 2012 National Report
http://feedingamerica.issuelab.org/resource/hunger_in_america_2010_national_report
Need Help?
http://feedingamerica.org/need-help.aspx
Philanthropy:
Volunteer
http://feedingamerica.org/getinvolved/volunteer.aspx
Advocate
http://help.feedingamerica.org/site/PageServer?pagename=advocacy_Take_Action&s_subsrc=Corporate%2520Opportunities
Take Action
http://help.feedingamerica.org/site/PageServer?pagename=advocacy_Take_Action&s_subsrc=Ways%2520to%2520Give

Corporate Opportunities
http://feedingamerica.org/get-involved/corporate-opportunities.aspx
Ways to Give
http://feedingamerica.org/ways-to-give.aspx

PSYCHOLOGICAL COUNSELING/HELP

American Psychological Association (APA)
is the largest scientific and professional organization representing psychology in the United States. Its membership includes more than 150,000 researchers, educators, clinicians, consultants, and students. APA works to advance psychology as a science and profession and as a means of promoting health, education, and human welfare.

Website:
http://www.apa.org/index.aspx
Contact Details:
750 First Street NE
Washington, DC 20002-4242
Phone: 1-800-374-2721
Need Help?
http://www.apa.org/helpcenter/index.aspx

Suicide Prevention Lifeline

is a 24-hour, toll-free, confidential suicide prevention hotline available to anyone in suicidal crisis or emotional distress.

By dialing 1-800-273-TALK (8255), the call is routed to the nearest crisis center in our national network of more than 150 crisis centers. The Lifeline's national network of local crisis centers provide crisis counseling and mental health referrals day and night.

Website:
http://www.suicidepreventionlifeline.org/
Contact Details:
Suicide Prevention Lifeline Locations
http://www.suicidepreventionlifeline.org/GetInvolved/Locator
Philanthropy:
Volunteer
http://www.suicidepreventionlifeline.org/GetInvolved/Volunteer
Donate
http://www.suicidepreventionlifeline.org/GetInvolved/Donate

PUBLIC POLICY

Center on Budget and Policy Priorities (CBPP) is one of the nation's premier policy organizations working at the federal and state levels on fiscal policy and public programs that affect low- and moderate-income families and individuals.

Website:
www.cbpp.org
Contact Details:
Center on Budget and Policy Priorities
820 First Street, NE, #510
Washington, DC 20002
Phone: (202) 408-1080
Philanthropy:
Donate
http://www.cbpp.org/donate/

Made in the USA
Monee, IL
08 November 2026

68156253R00094